T0087834

PANDEMIC! 2

PANDEMIC! 2

Chronicles of a Time Lost

SLAVOJ ŽIŽEK

Polity

This edition published by Polity Press, 2021

First published in the United States by OR Books LLC, New York, 2020

© Slavoj Žižek, 2020

All rights reserved. No part of this book may be reproduced or transmitted in any form or by any means, electronic or mechanical, including photocopy, recording, or any information storage retrieval system, without permission in writing from the publisher, except brief passages for review purposes.

9781509549061 Hardback
9781509549078 Paperback

To all those whose daily lives are so miserable that they ignore Covid-19, regarding it as a comparatively minor threat.

CONTENTS

INTRODUCTION

WHY A PHILOSOPHER SHOULD WRITE ABOUT BRINGING IN THE HARVEST

Something is rotten in north-by-northwest—and I don't mean Hitchcock's classic film but Gütersloh, a town in the north-by-northwest of Germany where in the middle of June 2020 more than 650 workers at the meat processing plant tested positive for Covid-19 and thousands are now quarantined. As usual, we are dealing with class division: imported foreign workers doing a dirty job in unsafe conditions.

The same bad smell is spreading all around the world. In late spring of 2020, something is rotting in the Southern state of Tennessee—tons and tons of unpicked fruits and vegetables. Why? Because 100 percent of the workforce at one farm in Tennessee, nearly 200 employees in total, tested positive for Covid-19 after one of the workers came down with the virus.[1]

This is just one of many examples of the threat posed by the pandemic to food supplies: products that must be hand-picked rely on hundreds of thousands of seasonal, mostly immigrant, workers who are moved around in crowded buses and sleep in cramped dormitories—an ideal breeding ground for Covid-19 infections. Cases are sure to climb since harvesting has to be completed quickly in the short window of time when the produce is ripe. These seasonal workers are in a very vulnerable position: their work is hard and insecure, their earnings are modest, their healthcare is as a rule inadequate, the immigration status of many is illegal. This is another example of the pandemic revealing class differences, the reality that we are not all in the same boat.

Cases like this abound all around world. There are not enough people to harvest fruits and vegetables in the south of Italy and Spain, tons of oranges are rotting in Florida, and similar problems are to be found in the UK, France, Germany, and Russia. Because of the pandemic, we are faced with a typically absurd capitalist crisis: thousands of eager workers cannot get work and sit idly by while tons of produce rots in the fields.

---

1. https://fortune.com/2020/05/29/farm-workers-test-positive-coronavirus-covid-19-tennessee/

INTRODUCTION

It is not just harvesting and distributing that are beset by difficulties—the growing of plants is also affected. Locusts are now ruining harvests from East Africa to the western parts of India, which are also threatened by droughts. Summing all this up: we are facing the prospect of considerable food shortages, if not outright hunger, and not only in Third World countries. The problem goes beyond we in the West having to pay a little bit more for our usual box of strawberries. The situation is not hopeless, but a fast and internationally coordinated response is needed—much more than calls for volunteers to help in the fields. Government organizations need to be involved in mobilizing people to avert the crisis.

At this point, I can hear the laughter of my critics (as well as some friends) who mockingly note how the pandemic means that my time as a philosopher is over: who cares about a Lacanian reading of Hegel when the foundations of our existence are threatened? Even Žižek now has to focus on how to bring in the harvest.

But these critics couldn't be more wrong. The ongoing pandemic hasn't just brought out social and economic conflicts that were raging beneath the surface all along; it hasn't just confronted us with immense political problems. More and more, it has become a genuine conflict of global visions about society. At the beginning of the crisis, it looked as if a kind of basic global solidarity, with the accent on helping those most threatened, would prevail; however, as John Authers puts it, this solidarity

3

has gradually "given way to a bitter factional and cultural battle, with rival moral principles hurled like metaphysical grenades. Different countries have taken antithetical approaches while the US has split itself almost into two nations, divided between those who wear masks and those who do not."[2]

This conflict is a serious existential one, so that one cannot simply make fun of those who refuse to wear masks. Here is how Brenden Dilley, an Arizona chat-show host, explained why he doesn't wear a mask: "Better to be dead than a dork. Yes, I mean that literally. I'd rather die than look like an idiot right now." Dilley refuses to wear a mask since, for him, wearing one is incompatible with human dignity at its most basic level.

That's why it is now entirely appropriate for a philosopher to write about bringing in the harvest: the way we deal with this problem ultimately depends on our basic stance toward human life. Are we, like Dilley, libertarians who reject anything that encroaches on our individual freedoms? Are we utilitarians ready to sacrifice thousands of lives for the economic well-being of the majority? Are we authoritarians who believe that only strong state control and regulation can save us? Are we New Age spiritualists who think the pandemic is a warning from Nature, a punishment for our exploitation of natural resources? Do we trust that God is just testing us and will ultimately help us to

2. See https://www.yahoo.com/finance/news/golden-rule-dying-covid-19-040107765.html

find a way out? Each of these stances rests on a specific vision of what human beings are. To that extent, in proposing how to tackle the crisis, we must all become philosophers.

1.

WHAT WE DON'T KNOW, WHAT WE DON'T WANT TO KNOW, AND WHAT WE CAN DO

I n the Marx Brothers' *Duck Soup*, Groucho (as a lawyer defending his client in court) says: "He may look like an idiot and talk like an idiot but don't let that fool you. He really is an idiot." Something along these lines should be our reaction to those who display a basic distrust of the state by seeing the lockdown as a conspiracy designed to deprive us of our basic freedoms: "The state *is* imposing lockdown orders that curtail our liberty, and it expects us to police one another to ensure compliance; but this should not fool us—we should really follow the lockdown orders. "

One should note how calls to abolish lockdowns come from opposite ends of the traditional political spectrum: in the US, they are propelled by libertarian Rightists, while in Germany, small Leftist groups advocate them. In both cases, medical knowledge is criticized as a tool for disciplining people, treating them as helpless victims who should be isolated for their own good. What is not difficult to discover beneath this critical stance is the attitude of not-wanting-to-know: if we ignore the threat, it will not be so bad, we'll manage to get through it . . . The US libertarian Right claims lockdowns should be eased in order to give people back their freedom of choice. That raises the question: what freedom? As ex–Labor Secretary Robert Reich wrote: "Trump's labor department has decided that furloughed employees "must accept" an employer's offer to return to work and therefore forfeit unemployment benefits, regardless of Covid-19. Forcing people to choose between getting Covid-19 or losing their livelihood is inhumane."[1] The "free choice" is, here, one between starvation and risking your life. The situation is reminiscent of that of an eighteenth-century British coal mine, wherein just doing one's job involved a considerable risk of loss of life.

But there is a different kind of ignorance that sustains the imposition of severe lockdown measures. It's not as simple as the state power exploiting the pandemic to impose total control—increasingly, I think that there is a kind of superstitious symbolic act at work here: a logic that says that if we make a strong enough gesture of sacrifice that brings our entire social life to a standstill, then maybe we can expect mercy. The surprising fact is how little we (and I include here the scientists) seem to know about how the pandemic works. Quite often we receive contradictory advice from the authorities. We get strict instructions to self-isolate in order to avoid viral contamination, but when the infection numbers start falling the fear arises that our actions are only making us more vulnerable to the anticipated "second wave" of the viral attack. Or are we counting on the hope that a vaccine will be found before the next wave? And

1. https://www.theguardian.com/commentisfree/2020/may/03/donald-trump-reopen-us-economy-lethal-robert-reich

as there are already different variations of the virus, will one vaccine cover them all? All the hopes for a quick exit (summer heat, herd immunity, a vaccine.) are fading away.

One often hears that the pandemic will compel us in the West to change the way we relate to death, to accept our mortality and the fragility of our existence—a virus comes out of nowhere and life as we know it is over. This is why, so we are told, people in the Far East are much better able to come to terms with the pandemic—for them, death is just a part of life, of the way things are. We in the West less and less accept death as part of life, we see it as an intrusion of something foreign that can be indefinitely postponed if you lead a healthy life, exercise, follow a diet, avoid trauma. I never trusted this story. In some sense, death is not a part of life, it is something unimaginable, something that shouldn't happen to me. I am never really ready to die, except to escape unbearable suffering. That's why these days many of us focus obsessively on the same magic numbers: how many new infections, how many full recoveries, how many new deaths. But, horrible as these numbers are, does our exclusive focus on them not make us ignore a much greater number of people dying of other causes like cancer or a heart attack? Outside the virus there is not just life; there is also plenty of dying and death. Perhaps it would be better to look at death rates comparatively: today, this many people died from Covid-19 while this many succumbed to cancer.

We should change our imaginary here and stop expecting one big clear peak after which things will gradually return to normal. What makes the pandemic so unbearable is that even if the full Catastrophe fails to appear, things just drag on—we are informed that we have reached the plateau, then things improve a little bit, but the crisis continues. As Alenka Zupančič put it, the problem with the idea of the end of the world is the same as with Fukuyama's end of history: the end itself doesn't end, we just get stuck in a weird immobility. The secret wish of us all, what we think about all the time, is only one thing: when will it end? But it will not end: it is reasonable to see the ongoing pandemic as announcing a new era of ecological troubles. Back in 2017, the BBC portrayed what awaits us as a result of the ways we intervene in nature, reporting that "Climate change is melting permafrost soils that have been frozen for thousands of years, and as the soils melt they are releasing ancient viruses and bacteria that, having lain dormant, are springing back to life."[2]

Viruses are undead, always ready to spring back to life, and the irony is that their "immortality" echoes the immortality promised by the latest developments in brain science. The pandemic occurred at a time when pop-scientific media outlets are obsessed with two aspects of the digitalization of our lives. On

2. http://www.bbc.com/earth/story/20170504-there-are-diseases-hidden-in-ice-and-they-are-waking-up

the one hand, much is being written about so-called "surveillance capitalism," a new phase of capitalism wherein total digital control is exerted over our existence by state agencies and private corporations. On the other hand, the media is fascinated by the topic of a direct brain–machine interface, or "wired brain." With this, when my brain is connected to digital machines, I can cause things to happen in the outside world just by thinking about them; and, further, when my brain is directly connected to another brain, another individual can directly share my experience. Extrapolated to its extreme, the wired brain concept opens up the prospect of what Ray Kurzweil called Singularity, the divine-like space of shared global awareness. Whatever the (dubious, for the time being) scientific status of this idea, it is clear that its realization will affect the basic features of humans as thinking/speaking beings. The eventual rise of Singularity will be apocalyptic in the complex meaning of the term: it will imply the encounter with a truth hidden in our ordinary human existence, i.e., the entrance into a new post-human dimension.

It is interesting to note that the extensive use of surveillance has been quietly accepted in many parts of the world: drones were used to tackle the pandemic not only in China but also in Italy and Spain. As for the spiritual vision of Singularity, the new unity of the human and the divine, a bliss in which we leave behind the limits of our corporeal existence, could well turn out to be an unimaginable nightmare. From a critical standpoint, it is difficult to decide which is a greater threat to humanity:

the viral devastation of our lives or the loss of our individuality in Singularity. The pandemic reminds us that we remain firmly rooted in bodily existence with all dangers that this implies.

Does this mean our situation is hopeless? Absolutely not. There are immense, almost unimaginable troubles ahead. There will be over a billion newly jobless people. A new way of life will have to be invented. One thing is clear: in a complete lockdown, we have to live off the old stocks of food and other provisions, so the difficult task now is to step out of the lockdown and invent a new life under viral conditions. Just think about the ways in which what is fiction and what is reality will change. Movies and TV series that take place in our ordinary reality, with people freely strolling along streets, shaking hands, and embracing, will become nostalgic images of a long forgotten past, while our real life will look like a variation of Samuel Beckett's late drama *Play,* in which three identical gray urns appear on the stage and from each a head protrudes, the neck held fast in the urn's mouth.

However, if one takes a naïve look at things (which is here the most difficult thing to do), it is clear that our global society has enough resources to coordinate our survival and organize a more modest way of life, with local food shortages compensated by global cooperation, and with global healthcare better prepared for the next onslaught. Will we be able to do this? Or will we enter a new barbarian age in which our attention to the health crisis will only enable conflicts like the reignited Cold

WHAT WE DON'T KNOW

War between the US and China, or the hot wars in Syria and Afghanistan, to continue out of sight of the global public? These conflicts operate in the same way as a virus: they drag on interminably. (Note how Macron's call for a world-wide truce during the pandemic was flatly ignored.) This decision as to which route we will take concerns neither science nor medicine, it is a properly political one.

2.

THE FIRST OF MAY IN THE VIRAL WORLD

Maybe, on the first of May, the moment has come to take a step back from our exclusive focus on the pandemic and consider what it and its devastating effects disclose about our social reality.

The first thing that strikes me is that, contra to the cheap motto "we are now all in the same boat," class divisions have exploded. At the very bottom of the hierarchy, there are those (refugees, people caught in war zones) whose lives are so destitute that Covid-19 is for them not the main problem. While they are still mostly ignored by our media, we are bombarded by sentimental celebrations of nurses on the frontline of our struggle against the virus—the Royal Air Force even organized a flypast in their honor. But nurses are only the most visible part of a whole class of caretakers who are exploited, although not in the way the old working class of the Marxist imaginary is exploited; as David Harvey puts it, they form a "new working class":

> The workforce that is expected to take care of the mounting numbers of the sick, or to provide the minimal services that allow for the reproduction of daily life, is, as a rule, highly gendered, racialized, and ethnicized. This is the "new working class" that is at the forefront of contemporary capitalism. Its members have to bear two burdens: at one and the same

time, they are the workers most at risk of contracting the virus through their jobs, and of being laid off with no financial resources because of the economic retrenchment enforced by the virus. The contemporary working class in the United States—comprised predominantly of African Americans, Latinos, and waged women—faces an ugly choice: between suffering contamination in the course of caring for people and keeping key forms of provision (such as grocery stores) open, or unemployment with no benefits (like adequate health care).[1]

This is why revolts recently erupted in the poor northern suburbs of Paris where those who serve the rich live. This is why, in recent weeks, Singapore has had a dramatic spike in Covid-19 infections in foreign worker dormitories. As one news report explains, "Singapore is home to about 1.4 million migrant workers who come largely from South and Southeast Asia. As housekeepers, domestic helpers, construction workers and manual laborers, these migrants are essential to keeping Singapore functioning—but are also some of the lowest paid and most vulnerable people in the city."[2] This new working class was here all along, the pandemic just propelled it into visibility.

1. https://jacobinmag.com/2020/4/
   david-harvey-coronavirus-pandemic-capital-economy
2. https://edition.cnn.com/2020/04/24/asia/
   singapore-coronavirus-foreign-workers-intl-hnk/

THE FIRST OF MAY IN THE VIRAL WORLD

To designate this class, Bruno Latour and Nikolaj Schultz coined the term "geo-social class."[3] Much of this class is not exploited in the classic Marxist sense of working for those who own the means of production; they are "exploited" with regard to the way they relate to the material conditions of their life: access to water and clean air, health, safety, Local populations are exploited when their territory is used for industrial agriculture or intensive mining to feed exports. Even if they don't work for foreign companies, they are exploited in the simple sense of being deprived of the full use of the territory that enables them to maintain their way of life. Take the Somali pirates: they turned to piracy because their coastal waters were depleted of fish by foreign companies' industrial fishing practices. Part of their territory was appropriated by the developed countries and used to sustain our way of life. Schultz proposes to replace here the appropriation of "surplus-value" with the appropriation of "surplus-existence," where "existence" refers to material conditions of life.[4]

As we are now discovering with the Covid-19 pandemic, even when factories are at a standstill, the geo-social class of caretakers has to go on working—and it seems appropriate to dedicate this first of May to them instead of to the traditional

3. See https://www.researchgate.net/publication/335392682
4. See Nikolai Schultz, "New Climate, New Class Struggles," in Bruno Latour and Peter Weibel (eds.), *Critical Zones: The Science and Politics of Landing on Earth* (Cambridge, MA: Cambridge MIT Press, 2020).

industrial working class. They are the truly over-exploited: exploited when they work (since their work is largely invisible), and exploited even when they don't work, in their very existence.

The eternal dream of the rich is of a territory totally separated from the polluted dwellings of ordinary people—just think about the many post-apocalyptic blockbusters like Neill Blomkamp's *Elysium*, set in 2154, where the rich live on a gigantic space station while the rest of the population resides on a ruined Earth that resembles an expanded Latin-American favela. Expecting some kind of catastrophe, the rich are buying villas in New Zealand or renovating Cold War nuclear bunkers in the Rocky Mountains, but the problem with a pandemic is that one cannot isolate from it completely—like an umbilical cord that cannot be severed, a minimal link with polluted reality is unavoidable.

3.

COVID-19, GLOBAL WARMING, EXPLOITATION—THE SAME STRUGGLE

From today's standpoint (at the end of June), the initial two months of the Covid-19 panic appear in an almost nostalgic light: true, we were in quarantine, but we expected this to last for a month or two before life would return to some kind of normal—even Dr. Fauci, director of the US National Institute for Allergy and Infectious Diseases, told Americans they could look forward to enjoying their summer vacations. We perceived quarantine as a limited time of exception, an almost welcome standstill in our all-too-busy lives affording us some peace with our families, some time to read books and listen to music, and to enjoy cooking meals, in the knowledge that it will be over soon. Now, we are in what some call the "whack-a-mole stage," with clusters constantly popping up here and there, not to mention the explosion of new outbreaks in countries like the US, Brazil, and India. Only now are we forced to accept that we are entering a new era in which we will have to learn to live with the virus. The situation is open, there is no clear indication of what direction the pandemic will take—or, as the German virologist Hendrik Streeck succinctly put it: There is "no second or third wave—we are in a permanent wave."[1]

1. https://www.welt.de/vermischtes/article210530869/Streeck-zu-Corona-Infektionen-Keine-zweite-oder-dritte-Welle-wir-sind-in-einer-Dauerwelle.html

But we are still all too focused on Covid-19 statistics, many of us regularly checking the numbers of infected, dead, and recovered on Worldometer. This fascination with the numbers automatically makes us forget the obvious fact that many more people are dying from cancer, heart attacks, pollution, hunger, armed conflicts, and domestic violence, as though if we get Covid-19 infections fully under control, the main cause of our troubles will disappear. Instead, human life will remain full of miseries and, in some sense, human life IS a misery that ends painfully, often with meaningless suffering.

Furthermore, the link between the Covid-19 pandemic and our ecological predicament is becoming ever more clear. We may get Covid-19 under control, but global warming will demand much more radical measures. Greta Thunberg was right when she recently pointed out that "the climate and ecological crisis cannot be solved within today's political and economic systems."[2] The same global mobilization that we were able to enact in response to the Covid-19 crisis is even more necessary with regard to global warming and pollution, but we continue failing to act in this direction, or, as Thunberg put it in a wonderful reversal of the title of Andersen's fairy tale: "The emperors are naked. Every single one. It turns out our whole society is just one big nudist party."

2. https://www.ecowatch.com/greta-thunberg-2646241937.html

COVID-19, GLOBAL WARMING, EXPLOITATION

Take a case of global warming that should convince even the greatest skeptics: the prolonged heatwave in Siberia that, in the first six months of 2020, caused wildfires, a huge oil spill, and a plague of tree-eating moths. As one news outlet reported, "Russian towns in the Arctic circle have recorded extraordinary temperatures, with Nizhnyaya Pesha hitting 30C on 9 June [. . .] Thawing permafrost was at least partly to blame for a spill of diesel fuel in Siberia this month that led Putin to declare a state of emergency. The supports of the storage tank suddenly sank."[3] Just think about all the long-frozen bacteria and viruses waiting to be reactivated with the thawing of permafrost!

The same goes for the link between Covid-19 and the anti-racist protests erupting around the world. The only effective answer to the ongoing debate about the assertion that "Black lives matter" (e.g., why shouldn't we instead say, "all lives matter"?), is a wonderfully brutal meme now circulating in the US, which depicts Stalin holding a poster that reads: "No lives matter." (I leave aside here the polemics about Stalinist murders in Australia that gave birth to this version of the meme.) The kernel of truth in this provocation is that there are things that matter more than bare life—is this not also the primary message of those protesting police violence against Black people? Black people (and those who support them) are not demanding

3. https://www.theguardian.com/environment/2020/jun/17/
   climate-crisis-alarm-at-record-breaking-heatwave-in-siberia

mere survival, they are demanding to be treated with dignity, as free and equal citizens, and for this they are ready to risk a lot, including sometimes their lives. That's why they gather to protest even when it increases the risk of spreading or contracting Covid-19.

Does this mean that Giorgio Agamben was right when he rejected state-imposed lockdowns and self-isolation as measures that imply reducing our lives to mere existence—in the sense that, when we follow the lockdown regulations, we demonstrate that we are ready to renounce what makes our lives worth living for the chance of bare survival? Do we have to risk our lives (by way of exposing ourselves to possible infection) in order to remain fully human? The problem with this stance is that, today, the main proponents of abolishing lockdowns are to be found in the populist new Right: its members see in all similar restrictive measures—from lockdowns to the obligatory wearing of masks—the erosion of our freedom and dignity. To this, we should respond by raising the key question: what does abolishing lockdowns and isolation effectively amount to for ordinary workers? That, in order to survive, they must go out into the unsafe world and risk contamination.

This brings us to the key point: the contradictory way the Covid-19 pandemic has affected the economy. On the one hand, it has forced authorities to do things that at times almost point toward Communism: a form of Universal Basic Income, healthcare for all, etc. However, this unexpected opening for

Communism is just one side of the coin. Simultaneously, opposite processes are asserting themselves violently, with corporations amassing wealth and being bailed out by states. The contours of corona-capitalism are gradually emerging, and with them new forms of class struggle—or, to quote Joshua Simon, writer and curator from Philadelphia:

> US cities have seen the largest rent strike in decades, at least 150 worker strikes and walkouts (most notably by Amazon warehouse workers), and hunger strikes in refugee detention facilities. At the same time, research shows that US billionaires increased their collective wealth by \$282 billion in just twenty-three days during the initial weeks of the coronavirus lockdown. We are forced to recognize the immense inequalities proliferating with the pandemic and lockdown, with people losing their jobs, with gigantic bailouts that overwhelmingly benefit the biggest corporations and the already extremely wealthy, and with the ways those deemed essential workers are forced to keep working.[4]

The main form of the new exploitation that characterizes work in the conditions of the pandemic (in the West) is, to quote Simon again, "the shifting of costs to workers. From people

4. https://socialtextjournal.org/periscope_article/the-sign-language-of-the-tiny-hands-of-the-market/

having no sick leave, to teachers using their broadband and laptops at home to teach, households are performing all reproductive and productive labour." In these conditions, it is no longer primarily the capitalist who owns the means of production and hires workers to operate them: "the worker brings with her the means of production. Directly, this happens with the Amazon delivery person or Uber driver bringing to work their own car, filled up with gasoline, with insurance and driver's license all taken care of." Simon evokes the poster held by Sarah Mason at an anti-lockdown protest: "Social Distancing Equals Communism." What we get when distancing is abolished is this apparent "freedom" of workers who own their means of production and run around on errands for the company while risking infection. The paradox here is that both of the main variants of the corona-economy—working at home in lockdown and running deliveries of things like food and packages—are similarly subsumed to capital and imply extra-exploitation.

So our reply to Sarah Mason should be: yes, and that's why we need social distancing. But what we need even more is a new economic order that will allow us to avoid the debilitating choice between economic revival and saving lives.

4.

WHY DESTROYING MONUMENTS IS NOT RADICAL ENOUGH

I t was widely reported in our media how on June 21, German authorities were shocked over a rampage of an "unprecedented scale" in the center of Stuttgart: four to five hundred partygoers ran riot overnight, smashing shop windows, plundering stores, and attacking police. Police (who needed four and a half hours to quell the violence) ruled out any political motives for these "civil war-like scenes," describing the perpetrators as people from the "party scene or events scene".[1] With bars and clubs remaining closed as a result of the Covid-19 pandemic, rioting broke out in public. Such incidents are not limited to Germany. On June 25, thousands packed England's beaches, ignoring social distancing. As one news site reported, "The area was overrun with cars and sunbathers, leading to gridlock. Rubbish crews also suffered abuse and intimidation as they tried to remove mountains of waste from the seafront and there were a number of incidents involving excessive alcohol and fighting."[2] One can easily discern in such violent outbursts a reaction to the immobility imposed by social distancing and quarantine— it is reasonable to expect that more acts like these will follow

1. https://www.theguardian.com/world/2020/jun/21/
   hundreds-run-riot-in-stuttgart-city-centre-after-drug-checks
2. https://edition.cnn.com/2020/06/26/football/liverpool-fans-
   police-criticize-gathering-anfield-title-win-spt-intl/

all around the world, and one should not restrain oneself from voicing the suspicion that the explosive worldwide anti-racist passion, although it is not just an outburst of meaningless violence but an expression of a progressive cause, obeys a similar logic: thousands threw themselves into anti-racist protests with a kind of relief that they were again able to tackle something that is not a stupid virus but "just" a social struggle with a clear enemy.

We are, of course, dealing here with very different types of violence. On the beaches of Bournemouth, people simply wanted to enjoy their usual summer vacation and reacted violently against those who wanted to prevent this. In Stuttgart, the enjoyment was generated by looting and destruction, i.e. by violence itself—this was a violent carnival at its worst, an explosion of blind rage with no clear emancipatory potential (although, as expected, some Leftists tried to read into it a protest against consumerism and police control). The (largely non-violent) anti-racist protests ignored the orders and prohibitions of public authorities on behalf of their struggle for a noble emancipatory cause. (These types of violence predominate in developed Western societies—we ignore here the most massive forms of violence that are already happening and will certainly explode in Third World countries like Yemen, Afghanistan, and Somalia. As the *Guardian* reported on June 27, "This summer will usher in some of the worst catastrophes the world has ever seen if the pandemic is allowed to spread rapidly across countries already convulsed by growing violence, deepening poverty and the spectre of famine."[3])

There is a key feature shared by the three types of violence in spite of their differences: none of them expresses a minimally-consistent socio-political program. It may appear that the anti-racist protests meet this criterion, but they fail insofar as they are dominated by the Politically Correct passion to erase traces of racism and sexism—a passion that gets all too close to its opposite, the neoconservative thought-control. A law approved on June 16 by Romanian lawmakers prohibits all educational institutions from "propagating theories and opinions on gender identity according to which gender is a separate concept from biological sex".[4] Even Vlad Alexandrescu, a center-right senator and university professor, noted that with this law "Romania is aligning itself with positions promoted by Hungary and Poland and becoming a regime introducing thought policing".[5] Directly prohibiting gender theory is of course an old part of the program of populist new Right, but it has been given a new push by the pandemic: a typical new Right populist reaction to the pandemic is that its outbreak is ultimately the result

3. https://www.theguardian.com/world/2020/jun/27/toxic-mix-of-violence-and-virus-sweeps-poorest-countries-warns-war-reporter-lyse-doucet

4. http://www.cdep.ro/pls/proiecte/upl_pck2015.proiect?idp=18210

5. https://www.euronews.com/2020/06/17/romania-gender-studies-ban-students-slam-new-law-as-going-back-to-the-middle-ages

of our global society in which multiculturalism and non-binary pluralism predominate—the way to fight it is, therefore, to make our societies more nationalist, rooted in a particular culture with firm traditional values.

Let's leave aside the obvious counter-argument that the pandemic is ravaging fundamentalist countries like Saudi Arabia and Qatar, and focus on the procedure of "thought policing" whose ultimate expression was the infamous *Index Librorum Prohibitorum* (List of Prohibited Books), a list of publications deemed heretical or contrary to morality by the Sacred Congregation of the Index, and which Catholics were therefore forbidden to read without permission. This list was operative (and regularly renovated) from early modernity until 1966, and everyone who counted in European culture was, at some point, included—in philosophy from Descartes and Kant, to Sartre and de Beauvoir. As my friend Mladen Dolar noted some years ago, if you imagine European culture without all of the books and authors that were at some point on the list, what remains is a wasteland. The reason I mention this is that I think the recent urge to cleanse our culture and education of all traces of racism and sexism courts the danger of falling into the same trap as the Catholic Church's index: what remains if we discard all authors in whom we find some traces of racism and anti-feminism? Quite literally all the great philosophers and writers disappear.

Let's take Descartes, who was at one point on the Catholic index but is also widely regarded as the philosophical originator of Western hegemony, which is immanently racist and sexist. We should not forget that the grounding experience of Descartes's position of universal doubt is precisely a "multicultural" experience of how one's own tradition is no better than what appears to us as the "eccentric" traditions of others: as he wrote in his *Discourse on Method*, he recognized in the course of his travels that traditions and customs that "are very contrary to ours are yet not necessarily barbarians or savages, but may be possessed of reason in as great or even a greater degree than ourselves." This is why, for a Cartesian philosopher, ethnic roots and national identity are simply *not a category of truth*. This is also why Descartes was immediately popular among women: as one of his early readers put it, *cogito*—the subject of pure thinking—has no sex. Today's claims about sexual identities as socially constructed and not biologically determined are only possible against the background of the Cartesian tradition—there is no modern feminism and anti-racism without Descartes's thought. So, in spite of his occasional lapses into racism and sexism, Descartes deserves to be celebrated, and we should apply the same criterion to all great names from our philosophical past: from Plato and Epicurus to Kant and Hegel, Marx and Kierkegaard. Modern feminism and anti-racism emerged out of this long emancipatory tradition, and it would be sheer madness to leave this noble tradition to obscene populists and conservatives.

The same argument applies to many disputed political figures. Yes, Thomas Jefferson had slaves and opposed the Haitian Revolution, but he laid the politico-ideological foundations for later Black liberation. And in a more general view, yes, in invading the Americas, Western Europe did cause maybe the greatest genocide in world history—but European thought laid the politico-ideological foundation for us today to see the full scope of this horror. And it's not just about Europe: yes, while the young Gandhi fought in South Africa for the equal rights of Indians, he ignored the predicament of Blacks—but he nonetheless brought to a successful conclusion the biggest ever anti-colonial movement. So, while we should be ruthlessly critical about our past (and especially the past that persists in our present), we should not succumb to self-contempt—respect for others based on self-contempt is always and by definition false. The paradox is that in our societies, the whites who participate in anti-racist protests are mostly upper-middle class whites who hypocritically enjoy their guilt. Maybe, these protesters should learn the lesson of Frantz Fanon who certainly cannot be accused of not being radical enough:

> Every time a man has contributed to the victory of the dignity of the spirit, every time a man has said no to an attempt to subjugate his fellows, I have felt solidarity with his act. In no way does my basic vocation have to be drawn from the past of peoples of color. [. . .] My black skin is not a repository for specific

values. [. . .] I as a man of color do not have the right to hope that in the white man there will be a crystalliza-tion of guilt toward the past of my race. I as a man of color do not have the right to seek ways of stamping down the pride of my former master. I have neither the right nor the duty to demand reparations for my sub-jugated ancestors. There is no black mission; there is no white burden. [. . .] Am I going to ask today's white men to answer for the slave traders of the seventeenth century? Am I going to try by every means available to cause guilt to burgeon in their souls? [. . .] I am not a slave to slavery that dehumanized my ancestors.[6]

If we reject the notion of the generalized guilt of white men, we should of course also show no tolerance for their continued Politically Correct racism, whose exemplary case is the infa-mous Amy Cooper video[7] that was filmed in Central Park. As Russell Sbriglia commented,

the strangest, most jarring part of the video is that she specifically says—both to the black man him-self before she calls 911 and to the police dispatcher once she's on the phone with them—that "an *African American* man" is threatening her life. It's almost as

6. Frantz Fanon, *Black Skin, White Masks* (New York, NY: Grove Press, 2008), pp. 201–206.
7. https://www.cnn.com/2020/05/26/us/ central-park-video-dog-video-african-american-trnd/

if, having mastered the proper, politically correct jargon ("African American," not "black"), what she's doing couldn't possibly be racist.[8]

Instead of perversely enjoying our guilt (and thereby patronizing the true victims), we need active solidarity: guilt and victimhood immobilize us. Only when we all act together, treating ourselves and each other as responsible adults, can we beat racism and sexism.

8. Private message from Russell Sbriglia.

5.

FATHER . . . OR WORSE

What first came to my mind when I heard news of the protests in Belarus was the well-known dialogue between a Scotland Yard detective and Sherlock Holmes in the story "The Adventure of Silver Blaze," about the "curious incident of the dog in the night-time": "Is there any other point to which you would wish to draw my attention?" "To the curious incident of the dog in the night-time." "The dog did nothing in the night-time." "That was the curious incident." Although one of the reproaches against Lukashenko was the government's poor handling of the Covid-19 outbreak, the topic was notably absent from public debates on the protests, such that one could imagine a journalist asking a specialist on Belarus: "Is there any other point about the Minsk protests to which you would wish to draw my attention?" "To the curious incident with the coronavirus in the Minsk main square." "But the coronavirus was barely mentioned there." "That was the curious incident." What Lukashenko and the protesters share is a dismissive stance toward Covid-19: the crowds in Minsk didn't seem to care about social distancing and very few masks were visible, while Lukashenko continually seeks to defy the dangers of Covid-19—he even boasted of holding the only Victory Day parades in the former Soviet Union on May 8. (One should nonetheless note that Belarus is handling the pandemic better than its neighboring countries.) No wonder freedom-loving liberals are enthusiastic about the events in Belarus, seen as proof that even the threat of Covid-19 is no match for a good old-fashioned mass protest. For a brief moment, at least, the pandemic was relegated to the background, and we returned to the well-known scenario of the masses toppling "the last dictator in Europe"—Minsk as a new Kyiv.

However, this joyful enthusiasm for democracy has its own blind spot. We should, of course, support the protests: Lukashenko is an eccentric authoritarian leader, a somewhat ridiculous figure who runs his state with an iron fist, arresting opponents and allowing very little freedom of the press—however, he cannot be dismissed as simply a failure. Benjamin Bidder wrote in an article entitled "Lukashenko's Disappearing Model of Society," "For a long time, he brought Belarus to a modest welfare—that was enough to make him highly popular even in the neighboring states. But his model of economy is in trouble."[1] Lukashenko achieved economic stability, safety, and order, with a per capita income much higher than in the "free" Ukraine, and distributed in a much more egalitarian way. But with one of his most important profitable enterprises—getting cheap oil from Russia and

1. https://www.spiegel.de/wirtschaft/belarus-alexander-lukaschenkos-schwindendes-geschaeftsmodell-a-0bfac8e5-b9ec-4aac-98bd-70851bce16a8

reselling it to the West—now coming to an end due to low oil prices, his time has run out.

The ongoing protests in Belarus are catch-up protests aimed toward rejoining Western liberal-capitalist normality; they do not directly tackle the severe problems that today plague developed countries themselves. One can therefore safely predict that if the protests are victorious, these problems will arise immediately after the initial enthusiasm passes, and the final outcome might well be a new, more national-conservative version of Lukashenko, a Belarusian Orbán or Kaczynski. That is to say, one should bear in mind the reason behind Lukashenko's relative popularity in previous years: he was tolerated, even accepted in some circles, precisely because he offered a safe haven against the ravages of wild liberal capitalism (corruption, economic and social uncertainty,) Now the situation is clear: a large majority wants to get rid of the tyrant. Problems begin *after* the people win—against whom do you protest in democracy? Since there is no clearly visible tyrant, the temptation is to search for an *invisible master* who pulls the strings (like the Jews who control the "deep state"). Lukashenko's affectionate nickname among his partisans is "batka" (father), and one cannot help but recall here the title of one of Jacques Lacan's late seminars: . . . *ou pire* (. . . or worse). Lacan is evoking here the phrase "*le pere ou pire* (the father or worse), implying a dire warning of how the final outcome of anti-patriarchal rebellions can be a leader worse than the deposed patriarch.

The protests shaking the world in the last few years clearly oscillate between two types. On the one hand, we have the catch-up protests that enjoy the support of Western liberal media; for instance, those in Hong Kong and Minsk. On the other hand, we have much more troubling protests that react to the limits of the liberal-democratic project itself, such as the Yellow Vests, Black Lives Matter, and Extinction Rebellion. The relationship between the two types resembles the well-known paradox of Achilles and the tortoise. In a foot-race with the tortoise, Achilles allows the tortoise a head start of, for instance, 100 meters. After some fine amount of time, Achilles will have run 100 meters, bringing him to the tortoise's starting point; during this time, the tortoise has run a much shorter distance, say 2 meters. It will then take Achilles some further time to run that distance, by which time the tortoise will have advanced farther; and then more time still to reach this third point, while the tortoise moves ahead. Thus, whenever Achilles arrives at a place the tortoise has been, he still has some distance to go before he can reach the tortoise. But let's just slightly change the temporal coordinates: let Achilles run 200 meters, and in the same unit of time the tortoise will cover only 4 meters and will thus be left far behind by Achilles. So the conclusion that imposes itself is: Achilles cannot ever reach the tortoise, but he can easily overtake it.

If we replace Achilles by "forces of democratic uprising" and the tortoise by the ideal of "liberal democratic capitalism", we soon realize that most countries cannot get close to this ideal, and that their failure to reach it expresses weaknesses of the global capitalist system itself. The only alternate option available to these countries is the risky move of reaching beyond this system, which of course brings its own dangers. Additionally, we are forced to realize that while pro-democracy protesters strive to catch-up to the liberal capitalist West, there are clear signs that, economically and politically, the developed West itself is entering what can only be called a post-capitalist and post-liberal era—a dystopian one, of course.

Yanis Varoufakis points out a key sign of things to come: when it was recently announced that the UK and US were entering their worst ever recessions, their stock markets reached record high.[2] Although part of this can be explained by simple facts (most stock market highs are driven by just a few companies that thrive, like Google and Tesla), the general tendency is that of the decoupling of financial circulation and speculation from production. (This is also mirrored by the rise of a new type of "subject supposed to know", an example of which is seen in a recent Yahoo report titled "Warren Buffett on Mind and Body" today, those supposed to dispense advice on various aspects of human life are not great scientists, artists, or productive inventors but financial speculators who embody universal wisdom and can give insight even into metaphysical questions). Netflix is exemplary here: while it loses money, it continues to expand.

2. Personal communication.

The true choice is thus: what kind of post-capitalism will we find ourselves in?

As for the state of democracy, it suffices to take a look at the cover stories in our media. In Poland, liberal public figures complain that they are becoming spectators to the dismantling of democracy. In the US, Obama has warned that Trump presents a grave threat to democracy itself, while Trump is signaling that he will not recognize the results of presidential elections if they are not in his favor. Does this not echo Lukashenko?

So let's wish all the luck to protesters in Belarus: if they win, Covid-19 concerns will return with a vengeance, along with all of the other related pressing issues from ecology to new poverty. They will need luck—and courage.

6.

SEX IN THE AGE OF SOCIAL DISTANCING

I n Ireland, the Health Service Executive issued guidelines about practicing sex in the time of Covid-19, and the two key recommendations are:

> Taking a break from physical and face-to-face inter-actions is worth considering, especially if you usually meet your sex partners online or make a living by hav-ing sex. Consider using video dates, sexting or chat rooms. Make sure to disinfect keyboards and touch screens that you share with others. Masturbation will not spread coronavirus, especially if you wash your hands (and any sex toys) with soap and water for at least 20 seconds before and after.[1]

This is reasonable common-sense advice for a time of a pan-demic that is spread by bodily contact, but one should note that it only concludes the process already occurring with the progres-sive digitalization of our lives: statistics show that today's ado-lescents spend much less time exploring sexuality than explor-ing the web and drugs. Even if they do engage in sex, isn't doing it in cyberspace (with all of the hardcore pornography on offer) much easier and more instantly gratifying? For this reason, the

1. https://www.sexualwellbeing.ie/sexual-health/sex-and-coronavirus

new US TV series *Euphoria* (described in publicity materials as following "a group of high school students as they navigate drugs, sex, identity, trauma, social media, love and friendship") almost portrays the opposite of the life of today's high schoolers. It is out of touch with today's youth and, for this reason, weirdly anachronistic—more an exercise in middle-aged nostalgia for how depraved the younger generations once were.

But we should take a step further here: what if there never was an entirely "real" sex with no virtual or fantasized supplement? Masturbation is normally understood as "doing it to yourself while imagining a partner or partners"—but what if sex is always, up to a point, masturbation with a real partner? What do I mean by this? In a comment in the *Guardian*, Eva Wiseman refers to "a moment in *The Butterfly Effect*, Jon Ronson's podcast series about the aftershocks of internet porn. On the set of a porn film an actor lost his erection mid-scene—to coax it back, he turned away from the woman, naked below him, grabbed his phone and searched Pornhub. Which struck me as vaguely apocalyptic."[2] She concludes: "Something is rotten in the state of sex." To this I would add the lesson of psychoanalysis: something is constitutively rotten in the state of sex—human sexuality is in itself perverted, exposed to sadomasochist reversals and, specifically, to the mixture of reality and fantasy. Even

2. https://www.theguardian.com/lifeandstyle/2019/dec/08/rough-sex-and-rough-justice-we-need-a-greater-understanding-of-consent

when I am alone with my partner, my (sexual) interaction with them is inextricably intertwined with my fantasies, i.e., every sexual interaction is potentially structured like "masturbation with a real partner," I use the flesh and body of my partner as a prop to realize and enact my fantasies. We cannot reduce this gap between the bodily reality of my partner and the universe of fantasies to a distortion opened up by patriarchy and social domination or exploitation—the gap is there from the very beginning. So I quite understand the actor who, in order to regain an erection, searched Pornhub—he was looking for a fantasmatic support for his performance. It is for this same reason that, as part of sexual intercourse, one will ask the other to keep talking, usually narrating something "dirty"—even when you hold in your hands the "thing itself" (the beloved partner's naked body), this presence has to be supplemented by verbal fantasizing.

This strategy worked for the actor because he was not in a love relationship with the actress—her body was basically a living sexbot for him. If he were passionately in love with his sexual partner, her body would have mattered to him since every gesture of touching her would disturb the core of her subjectivity. When one makes love with someone they truly love, touching their partner's body is crucial. One should therefore invert the common wisdom according to which sexual lust is bodily while love is spiritual: sexual love is more bodily than sex without love.

There seems to be nothing surprising in the title of a recent report in *Vice* magazine: "Covid-19 Lockdowns Have Led to a Huge Spike in Sex Doll Sales."[3] The obvious explanation seems sufficient: with all the social distancing imposed in response to the pandemic, people are avoiding direct physical contact. However, a detail mentioned in the report undermines this explanation: the vast majority of sex dolls are sold to married couples. How can this be? Duane Rousselle suggests the clue resides in the fact that "most of us feel more intensely connected to one another during the pandemic than ever before": the exploding of sex doll sales "is therefore exemplary rather of an attempt amidst the overly-connected nature of the pandemic to produce a barrier to the sexual relationship. These are not meant to overcome the sexual relationship but rather to 'plug up' and slow down the intensity of our access to real life sexual encounters."[4] Note the nice dialectical reversal at work here: the true problem of the pandemic is not social isolation but our excessive reliance on others, on social links—can we be any more dependent on others than we are during quarantine? For a typical married couple, all the usual excuses for avoiding sex are invalidated when they are quarantined ("sorry, no sex tonight, we have to visit friends or I have to finish some work"),

3. https://www.vice.com/en_us/article/7kpmpb/
   covid-19-lockdowns-have-led-to-a-huge-spike-in-sex-doll-sales
4. Personal communication.

and in a desperate search for an obstacle to the sexual duty, they interpose between themselves a plastic doll. The paradox is that what serves as an obstacle to the sexual relationship is a sexualized object par excellence.

Will, then, the ongoing pandemic limit sexuality and promulgate love in the form of distant admiration for a beloved who remains out of reach? The pandemic will definitely give a boost to digital sexual games without bodily contact. Hopefully, however, a new appreciation of intimate bodily contact will also arise out of the pandemic, and we will learn again the lesson of Andrei Tarkovsky for whom earth—inert, humid matter—is not opposed to spirituality but is its very medium. In Tarkovsky's masterpiece *Mirror*, his father Arseny Tarkovsky recites his own lines: "A soul is sinful without a body, like a body without clothes." Masturbating to hardcore images is sinful, while bodily contact is a path to the spirit.

7.

THE (NOT SO) BRAVE NEW WORLD OF PIGS AND MEN

On August 28, Elon Musk presented at a press conference in Los Angeles the first living proof of the success of his Neuralink project: what he referred to as "a healthy and happy pig" (how did he know the pig was happy?) with a brain implant that made its brain processes readable to a computer.[1] Musk emphasized the health benefits of Neuralink (skirting over its potential for an unprecedented control of our inner life), and announced that he is now looking for human volunteers. An ominous parallel with electroshock therapy is immediately evident here—first pigs, then men. Electroshock therapy was invented by Italian psychiatrist Ugo Cerletti in 1938 after he saw pigs being electric shocked before slaughter—seeing that this made them more docile, he was inspired to try the same treatment on humans.[2]

One must admit that this is a rather low blow against Musk. Both extremes are to be avoided in interpreting the significance of Neuralink: we should neither celebrate it as an invention that opens the path toward Singularity (a divine collective self-awareness) nor fear it as a signal that we will lose

1. See https://www.theguardian.com/technology/2020/aug/28/
   neuralink-elon-musk-pig-computer-implant
2. https://www.cchr.org/newsletter/volume4/issue3/10-facts-you-
   need-to-know-about-the-dangers-of-electroshock.html

our individual autonomy and become cogs in a digital machine. Musk himself falls into an ideological dream—here is the title and subtitle of a recent report in *The Independent*: "Elon Musk Predicts Human Language Will Be Obsolete in as Little as Five Years: 'We Could Still Do It for Sentimental Reasons'—Neuralink chief says firm planning to connect device to human brain within 12 months"[3] Even if we ignore the technical feasibility of this dream, just think what would happen to the process of erotic seduction if human minds directly (outside of language) shared experiences with one another. Imagine a seduction scene between two subjects whose brains are wired so that one's train of thought is accessible to the other: if my prospective partner can directly experience my intention, what remains of the intricacies of seduction games? Will the other not react with something like: "OK, I know you desperately want to f*** me, so why are you asking me all these stupid questions about the movies I enjoy and what I would like to have for dinner? Can't you feel that I would never have sex with you?" The whole thing would be over in seconds.

More fundamentally, the distance between our inner life (the movement of our thoughts) and external reality is the basis of our perception of ourselves as free: we are free in our thoughts precisely insofar as they are at a distance from reality, so that

3. https://www.independent.co.uk/life-style/gadgets-and-tech/news/elon-musk-joe-rogan-podcast-language-neuralink-grimes-baby-a9506451.html

we can play with them, create thought experiments, and engage in dreaming with no direct consequences in reality—no one can control our thought processes. Once our inner life is directly linked to reality so that our thoughts have immediate material consequences (or can be manipulated by a machine that is part of reality) and are in this sense no longer "ours," we effectively enter a post-human state. Neuralink should thus prompt us to raise not only the question of whether we will still be human if we are immersed in a wired brain, but also: what do we understand by "human" when we say this? I've dealt with these questions, inclusive of the new unheard-of modes of social control opened up by Neuralink, in my book *Hegel in a Wired Brain*. We mustn't forget that if I can directly regulate processes in reality with my thoughts (I just think that my coffee machine should prepare a latte macchiato and it happens), the implication is that the causal link also works in the opposite direction: those who control the digital machine that "reads my mind" can also control my mind and implant thoughts into it.

What is important for us today, in the epoch of the Covid-19 pandemic, is to recognize that the social (or, rather, bodily) distancing implemented in response to the virus and the Neuralink vision are supplementary to each other—how? Physical distancing as a defense against the threat of contagion has led to *intensified* social connectivity—not only within quarantined families but outside of them (mostly through digital media)—and outbursts of physical closeness (raves, partying, etc.) have erupted in reaction to both: the message of the rave is not just bodily closeness but also less social control and thus more distance from society at large.

What happened with the pandemic was not a simple shift from communal life to distancing but a more complex shift from one constellation of closeness and distancing to another. The fragile balance between communal life and the private sphere characteristic of pre-pandemic society is replaced by a new constellation in which the diminishing of space for actual/bodily social interaction (due to quarantines, etc.) doesn't lead to more privacy but gives birth to new norms of social dependency and control—don't forget that even drones were deployed to control us in quarantine.

The prospect of Neuralink thus ideally fits the vision of a new society in which human beings are bodily isolated, living in protective bubbles, and simultaneously sharing the same mental space—in our psychic lives, we will be closer to each other than ever before. What we need now is not only more physical proximity to others but more psychic distance from them.

8.

A NO-TOUCH FUTURE? NO, THANKS!

t may appear that the basic choice we have in terms of coping with the pandemic is one between the Trump way (a return to economic activity in the conditions of market freedom and profitability, even if this means thousands more deaths) and what our media decry as the Chinese way (total digitalized state control of individuals). However, in the United States, a third option is being propagated by the New York state governor Andrew Cuomo and ex-CEO of Google Eric Schmidt (with Bloomberg and Bill and Melinda Gates in the background). As Naomi Klein explains, the project announced by Cuomo and Schmidt proposes "to reimagine New York state's post-Covid reality, with an emphasis on permanently integrating technology into every aspect of civic life."[1] Klein calls this proposal the "Screen New Deal"; it promises safety from infection while maintaining all the personal freedoms liberals care for—but can it work?

In one of his meditations on death, the stand-up comedian Anthony Jeselnik says about his grandmother: "We thought she died happily in her sleep. But the autopsy revealed a horrible truth: she died during autopsy." This is the problem with Schmidt's autopsy of our predicament: it, and its implications,

1. https://theintercept.com/2020/05/08/andrew-cuomo-eric-schmidt-coronavirus-tech-shock-doctrine/ Quotes that follow are from this text.

make our predicament much more catastrophic than it currently is. Here is Klein's critical description of this vision of a "permanent—and highly profitable—no-touch future":

> It's a future in which our homes are never again exclusively personal spaces but are also, via high-speed digital connectivity, our schools, our doctor's offices, our gyms, and, if determined by the state, our jails. [. . .] for the privileged, almost everything is home delivered, either virtually via streaming and cloud technology, or physically via driverless vehicle or drone, then screen "shared" on a mediated platform. It's a future that employs far fewer teachers, doctors, and drivers. It accepts no cash or credit cards (under guise of virus control) and has skeletal mass transit and far less live art. It's a future that claims to be run on "artificial intelligence" but is actually held together by tens of millions of anonymous workers tucked away in warehouses, data centers, content moderation mills, electronic sweatshops, lithium mines, industrial farms, meat-processing plants, and prisons, where they are left unprotected from disease and hyperexploitation.

Two key points are immediately striking in this description. First is the paradox that those privileged enough to afford to live in the no-touch space are also the most controlled: their entire life is transparent to the true seat of power, an "unprecedented collaboration between government and tech giants [. . .] with public schools, hospitals, doctor's offices, police, and military all outsourcing (at a high cost) many of their core functions to private tech companies." Should these networks, which are the lifeblood of our existence, really be in the hands of private companies like Google, Amazon, and Apple—companies that, merged with state security agencies, will have the ability to censor and manipulate the data available to us or even to disconnect us from public space? Schmidt and Cuomo have called for immense public investment into these companies—should the public not then own and control them? In short, as Klein proposes, should they not be transformed into nonprofit public utilities? Without a similar move, democracy in any meaningful sense is de facto abolished, since the basic component of our commons—the shared space of our communication and interaction—is placed under private control.

Second, the Screen New Deal intervenes into class struggle at a very precise point. The ongoing viral crisis has made us fully aware of the crucial role of what David Harvey calls the "new working class": caretakers in all their forms, from nurses to those who deliver food and other packages, empty our trash bins, etc. For those of us who were able to self-isolate, these workers remained our main form of contact with others in their bodily form, a source of help but also of possible contagion. The Screen New Deal plans to minimize the visible role of this caretaker-class who have to remain non-isolated, largely unprotected, exposing themselves to viral danger so that we, the privileged, can survive in safety. Some even dream that robots will supplant people in caring for the elderly. But these invisible caretakers can strike back and demand better protection: in the meat-packing industry in the US, thousands of workers have already contracted Covid-19 and dozens died, and similar things are happening in Germany. New forms of class struggle will erupt here.

At the end of the Screen New Deal, if we bring this project to its hyperbolic conclusion, is the idea of a wired brain—of our brains directly (outside language) sharing experiences with one another in a kind of Singularity, or divine collective self-awareness. The realization of Elon Musk's Neuralink project could mean that human language is soon obsolete—does this vision not echo the situation of humans in *The Matrix*? Protected in our isolated bubbles, we will be more spiritually united than ever—a nightmarish vision if ever there was one.

During the protests that erupted in Chile in October 2019, a piece of graffiti was drawn on the walls that read: "Another end of the world is possible."[2] This should be our answer to the Screen New Deal: yes, our old world has come to an end, but a no-touch future is not the only option, another end of the world is possible.

2. I got this information from Juan Rodriguez.

9.

WHERE ARE GRETA AND BERNIE?

One of the facts that should surprise observers of the corona-scene is: where have Greta Thunberg and Bernie Sanders disappeared to? Except for a short note from Greta to say that she thinks she survived contracting Covid-19, one hears very little about the movement she mobilized. As for Bernie, although he advocated measures (like universal healthcare) that are now, with the pandemic raging, recognized as necessary all around the world, he is similarly nowhere to be seen or heard. Why did the pandemic have this effect on political figures whose programs and insights are today more crucial than ever?

In recent months, the topic of Covid-19 totally eclipsed ecological concerns and was only overshadowed in the last few weeks by the anti-racist protests that spread from the US all around the globe. The crucial ideological and political battle that is occurring today concerns the relationship between three domains: the pandemic, the ecological crisis, and racism. The establishment seeks to keep these three domains apart, and even to hint at tensions between them. One often hears that our main task now is to get the economy moving, and that to do this we should neglect ecological problems a little bit. One hears that chaotic anti-racist protests often violate social distancing and for that reason contribute to the spread of Covid-19. Against this line of reasoning, one should insist on the basic unity of the three domains: epidemics erupt from our unbalanced relationship with our natural environs, they are not just a health problem; in addition to being the overwhelming targets of police brutality, Black people are much more vulnerable to viruses than the white majority who can afford self-isolation and better medical care. We are thus dealing with crises that erupt as moments brought on by the dynamics of global capitalism: viral epidemics, ecological crisis, and racial unrest were all not only predicted but were already with us for decades.

As for the anti-racist protests, when Spike Lee was asked the question, 'Why did eight years of Obama fail to make substantial enough change to race relations in the US?' here is how he answered: "Very good question. But you have to understand: race relations—which have gotten worse—are a direct response to having a black president."[1] Why? Not because Obama was "not Black enough," but because he embodied the image of a Black American as advocated by the liberal Left, a Black American who succeeded while fully respecting the rules of the liberal game. The current protests are a brutal reply to the question: "Now that you've had a Black president, what more do you want?" It is our task to articulate this "more." Just remember that, during the eight years of Obama's presidency, the general tendency of the previous decades continued largely uninterrupted: the gap between the rich and the poor widened, big capital grew more

1. https://www.theguardian.com/film/2020/jun/12/spike-lee-race-relations-today-are-a-direct-response-to-having-a-black-president

powerful. In one of the episodes of *The Good Fight* (a follow-up series to *The Good Wife*), the heroine awakens in an alternate reality in which Hillary Clinton won the 2016 election, defeating Trump. But the result is paradoxical for feminism: there is no "Me Too," there are no widespread protests against the harassment of women because moderate establishment Left feminists fear that these may lead to Clinton losing male votes and not being ree-lected—plus, Weinstein is a large donor to the Clinton campaign. Did something similar, perhaps, happen with Obama?

There is a wonderful detail in Spike Lee's *Malcolm X*: after Malcolm gives a speech in a college, a white student approaches him and asks what she can do for the Black liberation strug-gle; he coldly answers "Nothing," and walks away. In citing this example, I have been criticized for implying that we whites shouldn't do anything to support the Black struggle; but my (and, I think, Malcolm's) point was more precise. White liberals should not act as if they will liberate Black people, but should rather support them in their own struggle for liberation—they should be treated as autonomous agents, not as mere victims of circumstances.

To return to our starting question: the disappearance of Greta and Bernie from the public domain does not mean that they were too radical for our time of viral crisis when more unifying voices are needed. On the contrary, they were not radical enough: they did not succeed in proposing a global new vision that would re-actualize their project in the conditions of a pandemic.

10.

WHAT MOVIE IS
NOW PLAYING OUT
IN REAL LIFE?

We often hear that what we are now experiencing with the Covid-19 pandemic is a real-life case of what was once depicted in Hollywood dystopias. The question is: what movie(s) are we now watching unfold in reality?

When, in the early weeks of the pandemic, I heard from friends in the US that gun stores had sold out their stock even faster than pharmacies, I tried to understand the reasoning of the buyers: they probably imagined themselves as a group of people safely isolated in their well-stocked house, defending it with guns against a hungry, Covid-infected mob, like in movies about the attack of the living dead. (One can also imagine a less chaotic version of this scenario, wherein a select elite is able to survive in secluded areas, as in Roland Emmerich's *2012*).

Another scenario, along the same catastrophic lines, came to mind when I read the following news item: "Death penalty states urged to release stockpiled drugs for Covid-19 patients. Top health experts sign letter saying badly needed medications used in lethal injections 'could save the lives of hundreds'."[1] I understood that the medication was needed to ease the pain

1. https://www.theguardian.com/us-news/2020/apr/13/death-penalty-states-coronavirus-stockpiled-drugs

of the patients, not to kill them; but, for a split of a second, I recalled the dystopian *Soylent Green* (1973), which is set in a post-apocalyptic overpopulated Earth wherein older citizens disgusted with the degraded conditions of life are given the choice to "return to the home of God." In a government clinic, they take a comfortable seat and, while watching scenes of pristine natural worlds, are gradually and painlessly put to sleep. When some US conservatives proposed that the lives of those over seventy years old should be sacrificed in order to save the economy and the American way of life, wouldn't the painless procedure staged in *Soylent Green* be a rather "human" way of enacting this?

But we are not yet there. When Covid-19 began to spread, most assumed that it would be a brief nightmare that would pass with the coming of warmer weather in the spring—the movie equivalent here was that of a sudden attack (earthquake, tornado,) whose function is to make us appreciate what a nice society we live in. (A subspecies of this narrative is that of scientists saving humanity at the last minute by inventing the cure (vaccine) to the contagion—the secret hope of most of us today.)

Now that we are forced to admit that the pandemic will be with us for some time (at least) and will profoundly change our lives, another movie scenario is emerging—that of a utopia masked as dystopia. Recall Kevin Costner's *The Postman* (1997), a post-apocalyptic mega-flop set in 2013, fifteen years after an unspecified apocalyptic event left a huge impact on human civilization and erased most forms of technology. It follows the story of an unnamed nomadic drifter who stumbles upon the uniform of an old US Postal Service mail carrier and starts to deliver mail between scattered villages, pretending to act on behalf of the "Restored United States of America." When others begin to imitate him, gradually, through this game, the basic institutional network of the United States emerges again. The utopia that arises after the zero-point of apocalyptic destruction resembles the United States of today, only purified of its post-modern excesses—a modest society in which the basic values of life are fully reasserted.

All of these scenarios fail to capture the really strange thing about the Covid-19 pandemic: its non-apocalyptic character. It is neither an apocalypse in the usual sense of the utter destruc-tion of our world, and even less an apocalypse in the original sense of the revelation of some hitherto concealed truth. Yes, our world is falling apart, but this process of disintegration just drags on with no end in sight. When the numbers of infected and dead rise, our media speculate about how far we are from the "peak"—are we already there? will it be in one or two weeks? We all eagerly track and await the peak of the pandemic, as if this moment will be followed by a gradual return to normality—but the crisis just drags on. Maybe we should gather the courage to accept that even if the vaccine against Covid-19 is discovered, we will remain in a viral world continually threatened by epidemics and environmental disturbances. We are now awakening from the dream that the pandemic will evaporate in the summer heat, and there is no clear long-term exit strategy—the only debate occurring is that concerning how to gradually weaken the lockdown measures. When, eventually, the pandemic recedes, we will all be too exhausted to take pleasure in it.

What possible scenario for the future can we arrive at from this "no-end-in-sight" narrative? The following lines appeared at the beginning of April in a major British daily, outlining one option:

> Radical reforms—reversing the prevailing policy direction of the last four decades—will need to be put on the table. Governments will have to accept a more active role in the economy. They must see public services as investments rather than liabilities, and look for ways to make labour markets less insecure. Redistribution will again be on the agenda; the privileges of the elderly and wealthy in question. Policies until recently considered eccentric, such as basic income and wealth taxes, will have to be in the mix.[2]

Is this a rehash of the British Labour manifesto? No, it's a passage from an editorial in the *Financial Times*. Along the same lines, Bill Gates calls for a "global approach" to fighting the disease and warns that, if Covid-19 is allowed to spread through

2. https://www.ft.com/content/7eff769a-74dd-11ea-95fe-fcd274e920ca

developing nations unhindered, it will rebound and hit richer nations in subsequent waves:

> Even if wealthy nations succeed in slowing the disease over the next few months, Covid-19 could return if the pandemic remains severe enough elsewhere. It is likely only a matter of time before one part of the planet re-infects another. [. . .] I'm a big believer in capitalism—but some markets simply don't function properly in a pandemic, and the market for lifesaving supplies is an obvious example.[3]

Welcome as they are, these predictions and proposals are all too modest: much more will be demanded. At a certain basic level, we should simply bypass the logic of profitability and begin to think in terms of the ability of a society to mobilize its resources in order to continue to function. We have enough resources— the task is to allocate them directly, outside the market logic. Healthcare, global ecology, food production and distribution, water and electricity supply, internet and phone connections— these are the priorities, all other things are secondary.

The task of allocating resources also concerns the duty and the right of a state to mobilize individuals. A major problem is now unfolding (not only) in France: it's time for the harvesting of

3. https://www.msn.com/en-gb/news/coronavirus/coronavirus-bill-gates-calls-for-global-agreements-on-masks-treatments-and-vaccines/ar-BBl2uCm4

spring vegetables and fruits, and usually thousands of seasonal workers come from Spain and elsewhere to do the job. Given that the borders are now closed, who will do it? France is already seeking volunteers to replace foreign workers, but what if there are not enough? What if direct mobilization is the only way?

As Alenka Zupančič concisely put it, if reacting to the pandemic in full solidarity would cause greater damage to our society and economy than the pandemic itself, is this not an indication that something is terribly wrong?[4] Why must there be a choice between solidarity and economy? Our answer to this false choice should be the same as: "Coffee or tea? Yes, please!" It doesn't matter what we call the new order we so desperately need—Communism or, to borrow from Peter Sloterdijk, "Co-immunism" (collectively organized immunity against viral attacks)—the point is the same.

This reality will not follow any of the above imagined movie scripts. We desperately need new scripts, new stories that can provide us with a kind of cognitive mapping, a realist and also non-catastrophic sense of where we should be going. We need a horizon of hope, we need a new post-pandemic Hollywood.

4. Private communication.

11.

DEATHS IN PARADISE

O ur world is gradually drowning in madness: instead of solidarity and coordinated global action against the Covid-19 threat, not only are agricultural disasters proliferating, raising the prospect of massive hunger (with locust invasions plaguing nations from Eastern Africa to Pakistan), political violence is also exploding, largely ignored by the media. How little have we read in the news about the military border clashes between India and China, in which hundreds were wounded? In such a desperate situation, one can be excused for escaping every so often into a good old formulaic crime series like the BBC's *Death in Paradise,* set on the imagined Caribbean island of Saint Marie. In a small community, dozens of murders are committed, all following the same formula: four main suspects are together at the time of the murder, each of them in view of the others, so how could one of them commit the crime? Our present reality continues to haunt us even when we escape into fiction, and parallels with the pandemic are apparent even in this crime drama.

In one of the later episodes of *Death in Paradise*, the police inspector discovers that the murderer had an assistant who helped him to erase the traces of his act, and that this assistant was none other than the victim himself—a man prone to bullying and humiliating others, but who also had pangs of conscience and regret. On a small island near Saint Marie, he runs a survival camp for four customers, and since only the five of them were on the island when the murder was committed, the culprit must be one of them. The inspector finds traces of somebody landing on the beach, walking to the site of the murder, then returning—as though a lone intruder came to the island specifically to kill the victim. However, some details disturb this image, and finally the inspector reconstructs what happened. The murderer was brutally humiliated and tormented by his victim in high school, which ruined his entire life. When he meets his tormentor at the survival camp, the latter doesn't recognize him, so he stalks him to a lone place in the forest and stabs him with a bamboo spear, shouting at him in despair that he ruined his life, before running away. Mortally wounded, but aware of the trauma he inflicted in his youth, the victim uses his last bits of his strength to arrange a scene that makes it look as though a foreigner landed on the island, thus exculpating the four others on the island, and then crumples down to die.

There is something noble in such a gesture, a trace of authentic redemption. But ideology finds a way to pervert even such noble gestures: it can compel the victim, not the criminal, to voluntarily erase the traces of the crime and even to present it as an act of his or her own will. Is this not what the thousands of ordinary people demonstrating for the end of the lockdown are doing in the paradise called the USA? A too quick return to "normality" advocated by Trump and his administration exposes many of them to the deadly threat of infection, but they nonetheless demand it, thereby covering the traces of Trump's (and capital's) crime.

In the early nineteenth century, many miners in Wales rejected helmets and other expensive protective equipment—although it greatly reduced the possibility of the deadly accidents that abound in coal mines—because the costs were deducted from their salary. Today, in the time of Covid-19, workers are being made to weigh a similar desperate calculation, a new inverted version of the old forced choice "money or life" (where of course you choose life, even if it is life in misery). If you choose life over money and isolate yourself at home, you won't survive, since to lose money is to lose life; instead, you must return to work to earn money and survive—but this life is curtailed by a threat of infection and death. Trump is not directly guilty of killing workers, but he is guilty of offering them a false choice according to which the only way to survive is to risk death, and he further humiliates them by creating a situation in which they have to demonstrate for their "right" to die at their workplaces.

One should contrast the anti-lockdown protests with the ongoing eruption of rage triggered by another death in the American paradise—that of George Floyd in Minneapolis. Although the rage of the thousands of (not only) Blacks protesting this act of police violence is not directly linked to the pandemic, it is easy to discern in the background the clear lesson of the statistics on Covid-19 deaths: Blacks and Hispanics are much more likely to die from the virus than white Americans. The pandemic has thus brought out the very material consequences of class differences in the US: it's not just a question of wealth and poverty, it is also quite literally a matter of life and death—both when we are dealing with the police and with health crises like the Covid-19 pandemic.

This brings us back to our starting point from *Death in Paradise*, to the noble gesture of the victim helping the perpetrator to erase the traces of his act—an act that, if not justified, was at least understandable as an act of despair. Yes, the anti-racist protesters are often violent, but we should show some of the same leniency toward this as does the victim toward his killer in the episode of *Death in Paradise*.

12.

NOW WE LIVE IN A STORE OF THE WORLDS

I may have finally discovered the movie that perfectly fits the moment we find ourselves in today: Paul Franklin's *The Escape* from 2017, based on the famous short story by sci-fi writer Robert Sheckley, "Store of the Worlds" (1958).[1] Although only 16 minutes long, the film is professionally made and has well-known actors in central roles (Julian Sands, Olivia Williams).[2]

Sheckley's story begins in what appears to be a destitute suburb in one of our megalopolises: "Mr. Wayne came to the end of the long, shoulder-high mound of gray rubble, and there was the Store of the Worlds. It was exactly as his friends had described; a small shack constructed of bits of lumber, parts of cars, a piece of galvanized iron, and a few rows of crumbling bricks." The eccentric old owner of the store explains to Wayne what he is selling: in exchange for all of their earthly possessions, he temporarily transposes his customers into an alternate reality where they can live according to their most intimate wishes. Wayne cannot decide whether or not to accept the offer, and the owner advises him to take some time to think it over. On his way home, Wayne continues to dwell upon the choice, and even afterwards, when he is immersed in the routines of

1. Available online at https://www.vice.com/en_us/article/a3ydpz/the-store-of-the-worlds
2. Available on https://vimeo.com/223579794

daily life—small problems with his wife and son, hectic events at work—the idea of returning to the Store and making the decision is always at the back of his mind. Time passes in this way, until he hears the owner's voice gently awakening him, asking him if the experience was satisfactory. Wayne puts his earthly possessions on the table—a pair of army boots, a knife, two coils of copper wire, and three cans of corned beef—leaves the Store and hurries down to the end of the lane: "Beyond it, as far as he could see, lay fields of rubble, brown and gray and black. Those fields, stretching to every horizon, were made of the twisted corpses of cities, the shattered remnants of trees, and the fine white ash that once was human flesh and bone."

The film adaptation retains the central twist of the story: the protagonist's return to ordinary daily life (haunted by the prospect of the decision) *was* the actualization of his desire—his reality is a miserable post-apocalyptic world in which he lost everything. One can easily imagine this narrative transposed into the present context of the Covid-19 pandemic: Wayne steps into the Store, an ultra-clean space in which one is obliged to wear a mask, hears the offer, and returns home to his ordinary, pre-pandemic life. He remains in this mundane alternate reality for a time, before he awakens and leaves the Store, finding the streets empty and the few people he meets wearing masks and protective shields.

While our situation is not quite so dire, we are in a similar predicament: our world is shattered and we dream not of some eccentric paradise (or hell) but of a return to normal social life without lockdowns, masks, and the constant fear of contagion. The situation is so messy and there are so many unknowns—no wonder we are prone to oscillate from one extreme to another. Until a week or two ago, we in Europe were obsessively following the rules of self-isolation; then something changed in people's attitudes and the threat is no longer taken so seriously— we go around without masks even if the rates of contagion are still high. (Maybe this reopening of social life is sustained by a desperate wager: the second wave of infections could be even worse, so let's enjoy a little bit of life while we can.) What we can be sure of is that the consequences of the pandemic for our mental health will be heavy: one analysis estimates that "As many as 75,000 Americans could die because of drug or alcohol misuse and suicide as a result of the coronavirus pandemic."[3]

We often read about how difficult it has become to do the proper work of mourning for all of those who are now dying, known and unknown to us, when the usual funeral rituals are not possible. But is there not another, more basic, kind of mourning pervading our social space? What we are really mourning is the abrupt end of an entire way of life. More precisely, we are not even ready to mourn this loss and remain stuck in melancholy because the old external reality is still here—it is just that, with

3. https://edition.cnn.com/2020/05/08/health/coronavirus-deaths-of-despair/

stores, restaurants, cinemas, and theaters closed, we cannot engage with it properly.

The problem we face today is that we cannot organize the coordinates of our desires; we need to reinvent them. Like Wayne in "Store of the Worlds," we desire to regain desire itself, the open situation of desiring. In this mess, a Store of the Worlds is already open, in the sense that we all know that we must do something and reinvent a new world. Trump is offering one world, the same old world of economic growth—and this only if we are willing to pay the price of many deaths. China is offering another world in which the state has total control over individuals. But, instead of browsing the limited options in this Store, we have to find the strength to turn and face reality. Georgi Marinov paints a convincing picture of our near future: "To avoid collapse of the social order, measures such as universal basic income, suspending rents, mortgages, debt payments and so on, nationalization of privatized components of the health systems and a number of other key industries, centralized governmental control of production and distribution of food, etc. will be needed."[4]

This list can be supplemented; for example, the isolation of workers in essential sectors (agriculture, energy, water supply, etc.) is needed to ensure their normal functioning. There is not

4. https://www.criticatac.ro/lefteast/coronavirus-scientific-realities-vs-economic-fallacies

currently a food crisis, but if Covid-19 spreads to rural areas and disrupts the growing and harvesting of crops, such a crisis will occur. In terms of further health measures, we should prepare for recurring, potentially long and strict quarantines. The typical answer to such suggestions is: the economy cannot sustain it. Here we must be precise: what economy cannot sustain the necessary health measures? The global capitalist economy that demands permanent self-expansion—the economy obsessed with rates of growth and profitability. As Marinov explains, "The instinct to 'not hurt the economy' brought us a ruined economy and a virus that has now spread everywhere, which will be very difficult to eradicate." As such, we must change our entire perspective: forget the car industry, fashion, and holidays in distant countries, we should calmly let this all fall apart and re-employ those who work in these industries in part-time roles elsewhere. We should build an economy that is able to function when society is forced to press "pause" and live in a prolonged standstill in which only the basics of life are provided.

The new world will have to be Communist in the sense of Marx's well-known maxim: "From each according to his ability, to each according to his needs." Are we not already moving toward this point? Not, of course, in the way Marx imagined it: a society of affluence in which everyone has a good life and works creatively. It will be a much more modest world in which everyone is provided with healthcare and enough food and resources to satisfy their basic needs, and everyone has to contribute to society in accordance with their abilities. Such a modest world can still be very satisfying spiritually and emotionally.

So, go and watch *The Escape* and use it to begin thinking about what kind of world we should build out of the ruins of the pandemic.

13.

YES, RED PILL . . .
BUT WHICH ONE?

A documentary on life in the Chernobyl zone after the nuclear accident shows an ordinary farming family who defied the orders to evacuate and continued to live in the area, forgotten by the state authorities. They don't believe in any mysterious nuclear rays—the land is there, and life just goes on. They were lucky in that radiation didn't seem to seriously affect them.

Does the situation of this family not bring to mind the famous scene from *The Matrix* in which Neo must choose whether to take the blue pill or the red pill? The blue pill would allow him to remain in what is known as ordinary reality, while the red pill would awaken him to the true state of things. "Reality" is of course a collective virtual dream manipulated by artificial intelligence, with our bodies being used as human batteries to power the AI machine. The Chernobyl farmers chose the blue pill and got away with it—or did they? From the perspective of the farmers themselves, it is the world around them that swallowed the blue pill and believed the grand lie about radioactive rays, while they refused to be seduced by this panic and remained firmly rooted in their daily reality.

One cannot help but notice how the metaphor of choosing the red pill and rejecting society's grand lies is, today, predominantly used by the new populist Right, especially with regard to Covid-19. Elon Musk recently joined their ranks, calling the mainstream response to the pandemic a "panic" and "dumb."[1] He exhorted his Twitter followers to "take the red pill," and his comment was quickly embraced by Ivanka Trump who announced that she had already taken the pill. One should notice the irony of Musk, who advocates a return to normality while at the same time publicizing his Neuralink project—the vision of which is to immerse human beings into a collective "wired brain" through which our minds directly communicate with one another, bypassing the need for language. Is this not the ultimate expression of "taking the blue pill": choosing a world wherein humans' bodily existence takes place in isolated cocoons, while their minds inhabit a shared virtual space?

Paradoxically, the populist new Right is here joined by some radical Leftists who likewise see in the Covid-19 panic a state conspiracy to impose total control over the population. Here is an extreme case: Giorgio Agamben claims that "professors who agree to submit to the new dictatorship of telematics and to hold their courses only online are the perfect equivalent of the university teachers who in 1931 swore allegiance to the Fascist regime."[2] This rejection of the resolute struggle against the viral pandemic is best encapsulated by the title of Olivier Rey's book on it: *L'Idolâtrie de la vie*—formerly, what we held as

1. https://www.nytimes.com/2020/05/19/technology/elon-musk-tesla-red-pill.html
2. https://medium.com/@ddean3000/requiem-for-the-students-giorgio-agamben-866670c11642

the Sacred was beyond life, we were ready to risk life for it; now, life itself is elevated to the role of the Sacred and we seem to be ready to sacrifice everything for bare life.

In the US, the struggle over the continuation of lockdowns is turning into a culture war: stores are hanging signs that read, ENTRANCE FORBIDDEN WITH MASKS! (not without but *with*!), while Trump has ordered all churches, synagogues, and mosques to open. My aim here is not to score cheap points against those who disavow the Real of the pandemic, but to elicit what pushes them to make this disavowal. "The pandemic threatens to develop into a perfect storm: the combination of three or more storms that multiplies their effects." While two of the storms— the health catastrophe and the economic crisis—are widely debated, another two—the unfolding international conflicts and the mental health crisis—receive much less attention.

We often read that the pandemic was a shock that changed everything, that nothing is the same now—true, but, at the same time, nothing has really changed; the pandemic only brought out more clearly what was already there. There is a lot of libertarian backlash against the idea of phones being used to locate individuals and prevent the spread of Covid-19, but state apparatuses have already been tracing our digital communications and phone calls for years—at least now they are using these capacities openly, to our benefit, and to ascertain specific data (our location). Much more concerning is the recent turn in the

tensions between China and the US, which were already height-
ened before the pandemic.

China is now seeking to tighten its control over Hong Kong
with a new security law that would allow Beijing to take aim
at the protests that have roiled the semiautonomous city. This
measure, the most aggressive one since Beijing took over Hong
Kong in 1997, should be interpreted alongside another fact that
is much less reported on. For the first time since Xi took over in
2013, the Taiwan section of the State Council annual report does
not include any mention of the "1992 Consensus," "One Country
Two Systems," "peace," or "peaceful unification." This is a major
departure from the past that might indicate that Beijing has
given up on the idea of a peaceful unification with Taiwan; for
if China succeeds in Hong Kong, the violent takeover of Taiwan
could be its next step, and this could lead to a full scale Pacific
war. Yes, Taiwan and Hong Kong are parts of China, but is this
the moment to pose military threats? Recall also that the news
that Israel plans to annex parts of the West Bank, and that the
US is considering restarting nuclear weapons tests. And many
other states are using the pandemic to more ruthlessly pursue
their usual aggressive politics. We live in a mad world in which
nobody seems ready to do the rational thing and adopt a truce
for the duration of the pandemic.

Madness brings us to the fourth, no less ominous, storm,
which is collective madness itself, or the looming collapse of
our mental health. Signs are already multiplying: eight in ten

YES, RED PILL . . . BUT WHICH ONE?

Italians said they need psychological support to overcome the pandemic; in Spain, half of the children in metropolitan areas have nightmares; in the US, tens of thousands of suicides are expected. This trend should not surprise us: the very fundamentals of our daily lives are disappearing. One should never underestimate the shattering effect of seeing one's daily customs collapse—mundane things like after-work drinks at the pub. George Orwell understood (see, for instance, 'The Moon Under Water' (1946)) pubs to be the key element of socializing for the lower classes, the place where their common mores were asserted, and it is doubtful if pub life will ever return as we knew it. Lacan called the space of common customs the "big Other," the symbolic substance of our lives, and psychotic breakdown looms when this big Other begins to disintegrate: the horror does not reside in our transgressions of social customs; rather, it erupts when we become aware that these customs are falling apart, that we have no firm ground to rely on.

Taking the true Red Pill means gathering the strength to confront the threat of these storms. We can do it because, to a considerable degree, they depend on us, on how we act and react in these difficult times. Let's not dream about a return to the old normality, but let us also abandon any dreams of entering a new post-human era of collective spiritual existence. The ongoing pandemic makes us aware that we are rooted in our individual bodies, and it is at this level that we should engage in the struggle.

14.

SIMPLE THINGS THAT ARE HARD TO DO

Traditional Marxists distinguished between Communism proper and Socialism as its initial, lower stage (where money and state still exist and workers receive wages, etc.) In the Soviet Union, there was a debate in 1960 about how far they'd come in this regard, and the conclusion was that, although they were not yet in full Communism, neither were they still in the lower stage (Socialism); so they introduced a further distinction between the lower and higher stages of Socialism. Is not something similar occurring today with the Covid-19 pandemic? Until about a month ago, our media was full of warnings about a second, stronger viral wave predicted to arrive in the fall and winter. With numbers of infections now spiking again everywhere, some claim that this is not yet the second wave, but only an intensification of the ongoing first wave.

This classificatory confusion only confirms that the situation with Covid-19 is getting serious, with cases erupting again all around the world. The time has come for us to take seriously simple truths like the one recently announced by the Director-General of the World Health Organization, Tedros Adhanom Ghebreyesus: "The greatest threat we face now is not the virus itself. Rather, it's the lack of leadership and solidarity at the global and national levels. We cannot defeat this pandemic as a divided world. The COVID-19 pandemic is a test of global solidarity and global leadership. The virus thrives on division, but is thwarted when we unite."[1] To take this truth seriously means that one should take into account not only international divisions, but also the class divisions within each country. As Philip Alston wrote in the *Guardian*: "The coronavirus has merely lifted the lid off the pre-existing pandemic of poverty. Covid-19 arrived in a world where poverty, extreme inequality and disregard for human life are thriving, and in which legal and economic policies are designed to create and sustain wealth for the powerful, but not end poverty."[2] Conclusion: we cannot contain the viral pandemic without also attacking the pandemic of poverty.

How to do this is, in principle, easy; we have the means and resources to restructure healthcare so that it serves the needs of the people in a time of crisis. However, to quote the last line of Brecht's "In Praise of Communism" from his play *The Mother*: "Er ist das Einfache, das schwer zu machen ist." ("It is the simple thing, that is so hard to do.") There are many obstacles that make it so hard to do, above all the global capitalist order, but I want to focus here on an ideological one—in the sense of the semi-conscious, even unconscious, stances, prejudices, and

1. https://www.npr.org/sections/coronavirus-live-
   updates/2020/07/09/889411047/lack-of-unity-is-a-bigger-
   threat-than-coronavirus-who-chief-says-in-emotional-sp

2. https://www.theguardian.com/global-development/2020/jul/11/
   covid-19-has-revealed-a-pre-existing-pandemic-of-poverty-
   that-benefits-the-rich

SIMPLE THINGS THAT ARE HARD TO DO

fantasies that regulate our lives also (and especially) in times of crisis. What is needed is a psychoanalytic theory of ideology.

In my work, I often refer to a series of Luis Buñuel's films that are built around the same central motif which Buñuel calls the "non-explainable impossibility of the fulfilment of a simple desire." In *L'Age d'Or*, the couple wants to consummate their love but are again and again prevented by some stupid accident; in *The Criminal Life of Archibaldo de la Cruz*, the hero wants to accomplish a simple murder, but all of his attempts fail; in *The Exterminating Angel*, after the conclusion of a party, a group of rich people cannot cross the threshold to leave the house; in *The Discreet Charm of the Bourgeoisie*, two couples want to dine together but unexpected complications always prevent the accomplishment of this simple wish; and, finally, in *That Obscure Object of Desire*, we have the paradox of a woman who, through a series of tricks, continually postpones the final moment of reunion with her old lover. Our reaction to the Covid-19 pandemic is quite similar: we all somehow know what has to be done, but a strange fate prevents us from doing it.

With Covid-19 infections again on the rise, new restrictive measures are being announced, but this time accompanied by the implicit (and at times explicit) proviso that there will be no return to a full lockdown—public life will go on. This proviso echoes a spontaneous outcry from many people: "We cannot take it (full lockdown) again! We want normal life back!" Why? Was the lockdown—to turn around Benjamin's "dialectics in a standstill"—a standstill without dialectics? Our social life is not at a standstill when we have to obey rules of isolation and quarantine—in moments of (what may appear to be) stillness, things are radically changing. The rejections of the lockdown are a rejection not of stillness but of change.

To ignore this means nothing less than a kind of collective psychosis. I hear in the outcries against lockdown an unexpected confirmation of Jacques Lacan's claim that *normality is a version of psychosis*. To demand a return to normality today implies a psychotic foreclosure of the Real of the virus—we go on acting as if the infections are not really taking place. Look at Donald Trump's latest speeches: although he knows the true scope of the pandemic, he speaks and acts as if he doesn't—ferociously attacking "Leftist Fascists" as the main threat facing the US today, and so on. But Trump is much less of an exception than we might think—we regularly read in the news that, in spite of new spikes in infections, the reopening of economy and society continues. In an unsurpassably ironic twist, the return to normality thus becomes the supreme psychotic gesture, the sign of collective madness.

This, of course, is not the whole truth about the psychic impact of the pandemic. In an epoch of crisis, the big Other (the substantial symbolic order that regulates our interactions) is simultaneously disintegrating, displaying its inefficiency, and tightening its grip (bombarding us with precise orders dictating our behavior). That is to say, psychotic foreclosure is not the only, or even the predominant, reaction to the pandemic. There is also the widespread obsessional stance, with many of us enjoying the protective rituals we practice to ward off the danger of infection.[3] We compulsively wash our hands, refrain from touching others and even ourselves, clean every surface in our homes, etc. This is how obsessionals act: since the Thing-Enjoyment is prohibited, they perform a reflexive turn and start to enjoy the very measures that keep the Thing-Enjoyment at a proper distance. Or, as Conor McCormack put it succinctly, linking common reactions to the pandemic with clinical structures: "Melancholia: It doesn't matter, I'm already dead. Schizophrenia: I hadn't noticed. Paranoia: I knew this was going to happen. Obsessional Neurosis: We'll all be okay if we follow the rules. Hysteria: Who's in charge here anyway?"[4]

This classificatory complexity of the psychic effects of the Covid-19 pandemic gets further complicated by the deeply ambiguous way our knowledge about the pandemic will affect its reality. Hegel didn't just say that we learn nothing from history, he said that the only thing we can learn from history is that there is nothing to learn from it. Of course we "learn from history" in the sense of reacting to past catastrophes and including them in our frameworks for a possible better future. After the horror of

3. I owe this point to Matthew Flisfeder, personal communication.
4. https://poddtoppen.se/podcast/1299863834/why-theory/
   coronavirus-and-its-discontents

the First World War, for instance, people were utterly horrified and they formed the League of Nations to prevent future wars—but it was nonetheless followed by the Second World War. I am here a Hegelian pessimist: every work of mourning, every symbolization of a catastrophe misses something and thus opens a path toward a new catastrophe. And it doesn't help if we know the danger that lies ahead. Take the myth of Oedipus: Oedipus's parents knew what would happen and the catastrophe occurred because they tried to avoid it. Without the prophecy that told them what would happen, there would have been no catastrophe. Our acts are never self-transparent, we never fully know what we are doing or what the effects will be. Hegel was aware of this, and what he called "reconciliation" is not a triumph of reason but the acceptance of the tragic dimension of our activity: we have to accept humbly the consequences of our acts, even if we didn't intend them. Russian Communists didn't want Stalinist terror, it was not part of their plan, but it happened and they were in some sense responsible. What if it is the same with the Covid-19 pandemic? What if some of the measures we take to fight it give birth to new catastrophes?

This is how we should apply Hegel's idealism to the reality of the pandemic. Here also, we should bear in mind Lacan's claim that there is no reality without a fantasmatic support. Fantasies provide the frame for what we experience as reality—the Covid-19 pandemic as a fact of our social reality is therefore also a mixture of fantasies and the real: the whole frame for how we perceive and react to the virus is sustained by different fantasies—about the nature of the virus itself, about the causes of its social impact, etc. The fact that Covid-19 almost brought the world to a standstill at a time when many were already dying of pollution, hunger, and war, clearly indicates this fantasmatic dimension: we tend to forget that there are people for whom Covid-19 is a minor issue.

Does this mean that there is no hope? Étienne Balibar said in reply to me (during a Birkbeck Summer School debate): "The idea that just because the crisis is a 'great' crisis (which I would agree with), all the 'struggles' are potentially merging into a unique revolutionary movement (provided we cry 'unite! unite!' loud enough), strikes me as a little childish. There remain some obstacles! People must survive first. " But I think that something like a new form of Communism will have to emerge precisely if we want to survive! If the last few weeks have demonstrated anything, it is that global capitalism cannot contain the Covid-19 crisis. Why not? As Todd McGowan pointed out, capitalism is, in its core, sacrificial—instead of immediately consuming the profit one should reinvest it, full satisfaction is forever postponed.[5] In the finale of Mozart's opera, *Don Giovanni* triumphantly sings: "Giacché spendo i miei danari, io mi voglio divertir." ("Since I spend my money freely, I want to be amused.") It is difficult to imagine a more anti-capitalist motto—a capitalist doesn't spend

5. Todd McGowan, personal communication.

his money to be amused but to get *more* money. However, this sacrifice is not experienced as such, it is concealed: he sacrifices now in order to later profit. With the pandemic, the sacrificial truth of capitalism was exposed—we are openly solicited to sacrifice (at least parts of) our lives NOW in order to keep the economy going, I am referring here to the demand of some of Trump's followers that people over sixty years old should accept death in order to save the capitalist way of life. Of course, workers in dangerous professions (miners, steelworkers, whale hunters) have risked their lives for centuries—not to mention the horrors of colonization—but the risk is now directly apparent, and not only for the poor. Can capitalism survive this shift to a daily life in which we are much more exposed to sudden death? I don't think it can: it undermines the logic of endlessly postponed enjoyment that enables it to function.[6]

The obverse of the incessant capitalist drive to produce ever increasing, newer, and different objects are the growing piles of useless waste—from mountains of used cars and computers to the famous airplane "resting place" in the

---

6. Let's take the latest example of how capital tries to accommodate itself to the Covid-universe: "Emirates has become the first airline to offer free Covid-19 insurance as it tries to get people flying again. Passengers will be covered for medical treatment, hotel quarantine, and even their funeral if they catch the coronavirus while travelling." The last point obviously doesn't fit the series of insurances since it ridiculously misfires: if I die I am dead, so why should I care for the cost of my funeral?

SIMPLE THINGS THAT ARE HARD TO DO

Mojave desert. In these ever-growing piles of inert, dysfunctional "stuff," one can, as it were, perceive the capitalist drive at rest. And didn't we also perceive this recently when, with the Covid-19 quarantines, our daily lives came to a halt? We suddenly saw the buildings and objects that we used every day—stores, cafeterias, buses, trains, and planes—just resting there, closed, deprived of their function. Was this not a kind of epoché (in the Husserlian sense of suspension of use) imposed on us in our actual life? Such moments should make us think: is it really worth returning to the smooth functioning of the same system?

However, the true ordeal is not so much the lockdowns and isolation, it begins now, as our societies are setting in motion again. I've already compared the effect of Covid-19 on the global capitalist order to the "Five Point Palm Exploding Heart Technique" from the final scene of Tarantino's *Kill Bill 2*. The move consists of a combination of five strikes with one's fingertips to five different pressure points on the target's body: the target can go on living so long as he doesn't move, but once he stands up and takes five steps, his heart explodes. Is this not how the Covid-19 pandemic affected global capitalism? The state of lockdown and isolation is relatively easy to sustain because we are aware that it is temporary, akin to taking a break; problems arise the moment we emerge from this and have to invent a new form of life—since there is no return to the old. In other words, the really difficult time is coming *now*.

In a not-yet-published essay, "Present Tense 2020," W.J.T. Mitchell reads the temporality of epidemics through the lenses of the Ancient Greek triad of Chronos, Aion, and Kairos. Kronos personifies the implacable linear time that leads inexorably toward the death of every living thing. Aeion is the god of circular time, of the seasons and the cycle of the zodiac, and of the eternal return as represented by the serpent with its tail in its mouth. Kairos has a double aspect of threat and promise—in Christian theology, it is the moment of fateful decision, the moment when "newness comes into the world," as in the birth of Christ.

Like most epidemics, the Covid-19 pandemic is largely interpreted in terms of Chronos or Aion: as an event in the linear run of things, a low point that, like a bad season, will sooner or later turn around. What I am hoping is that the pandemic will follow the logic of Kairos: a catastrophe that will compel us to find a new beginning. For many liberals, the unexpected appearance of Trump was a moment of Kairos: something new that shattered the foundations of the established order. But I think that Trump is just a symptom of what was already wrong in our societies, and we are still waiting for the new to emerge.

If we don't invent a new mode of social life, our situation will not be just a little bit worse, but much worse. Again, my hypothesis is that the Covid-19 pandemic announces a new epoch in which we will have to rethink everything, inclusive of the basic meaning of being human—and our actions should follow our thinking. Perhaps today we should invert Marx's Thesis XI on Feuerbach: in the twentieth century, we tried to change the world too rapidly, and the time has come to interpret it in a new way.

(NO TIME) TO CONCLUDE: THE WILL NOT TO KNOW

U p until now, some of us were desperately clinging to the hope that countries somehow associated with Socialism are better at containing the pandemic—not only those countries in which a Communist party still holds power like China, Vietnam, and Cuba, but also those with an entrenched social democratic tradition like those of Scandinavia. But cracks are emerging even in this edifice. The story that repeats itself again and again is that of a country that prepared itself well for the pandemic, and just when it seemed the virus was contained, it began to explode again.

The ultimate example of this is New Zealand. Even I, an old hardened Marxist cynic, followed the statistics every day with the hope that there would be no new cases in New Zealand. However, on August 11, New Zealand recorded four new cases of Covid-19 after 102 days without any community transmission, and a week later there were dozens of new cases each day. The lesson is clear: the New Zealand of our fantasies, the safe haven with no Covid-19, doesn't exist. In the short term, I wish New Zealand (one of my favorite countries) all the best, and I fully support all of its measures to contain the virus. In the long term, however, it is increasingly clear that only a global approach will work.

The predominant reaction to a rise in new cases just when the situation seems under control is not panic, but acceptance: even if the number of infected and dead is rising, many countries are trying to impose an appearance of normality. The World Health Organization warned of the risk of "response fatigue" given the socio-economic pressures on countries,[1] and we can already see this fatigue in the news: reports on Covid-19 are now preceded by other items (the contested elections in Belarus, the Barcelona–Bayern soccer match, Kamala Harris,) but there is something fake about this shift in attention—as if we are desperately attempting to avoid the true trauma that is, still, Covid-19. Furthermore, this weird fatigue is accompanied by protests and other forms of social disobedience—the headline of a recent report in the *Guardian* says it all: "Protests predicted to surge globally as Covid-19 drives unrest. New analysis finds economic shock of pandemic coupled with existing

1. https://www.ctvnews.ca/health/coronavirus/who-says-pandemic-will-likely-be-lengthy-warns-of-response-fatigue-1.5048701

(NO TIME) TO CONCLUDE

grievances makes widespread public uprisings 'inevitable.'"[2] The Red Cross has also warned of huge post-Covid migrations, another cause of unrest.[3] In China, there are indications of a threat of food shortages leading to widespread hunger, with Xi Jinping recently targeting "food waste" by issuing an order that limits the number of dishes restaurant customers may order.[4] Countries from Pakistan and India to France and Germany face a similar threat, with gigantic amounts of agricultural products being destroyed by locusts and rodents, or otherwise left to rot in the fields due to labor shortages.

Isn't it becoming clear that today, when a persistent pandemic is accompanied by a series of other major threats, we need to implement—though toward radically opposite ends— what the Nazis called "totale Mobilmachung" (total mobilization)? J. G. Fichte, in his *The Closed Commercial State* (1800), was perhaps the first to point in this direction. And, not unsurprisingly, his book is largely ignored or dismissed as proto-totalitarian (Karl Popper himself lists Fichte among the enemies of the "open society.") The first to criticize Fichte along these

2. https://www.theguardian.com/global-development/2020/jul/17/protests-predicted-to-surge-globally-as-covid-19-drives-unrest

3. https://www.theguardian.com/world/2020/jul/24/global-report-red-cross-warns-of-big-post-covid-19-migration-as-who-hits-back-at-us

4. https://www.theguardian.com/world/2020/aug/13/operation-empty-plate-xi-jinping-makes-food-waste-his-next-target

lines was none other than Hegel, who mocks the idea of a state that totally controls the actions and movements of its citizens. Today, however, such control is not only easily accomplished thanks to the digitalization of our societies but, as the pandemic has shown, is sometimes necessary. So, why not courageously rehabilitate the entire lineage of anti-liberal thinkers of the "closed" society (beginning with Plato)? In today's global liberal economy, Fichte's project of the re-politicization of economy is more important than ever. As Diego Fusaro points out, Fichte

> presents a concept that, on the one hand, plays a role of primary importance for a critique of the "liberal liberty" and, on the other hand, allows for a critical understanding of the aporias of today's "neoliberal condition". / The *Handelsanarchie* destroys the primacy of the human over things, of politics over economy, and produces what Carl Schmitt defined as "depoliticization", i.e. the deprivation of politics and its reduction to a mere *ancilla oeconomiae*. / Paraphrasing the well-known Carl von Clausewitz's formula, politics is now debased and reconfigured to be a mere continuation of economy by other means. [. . .] this is the mortiferous condition in which Europe has fallen into: a continent now debased as an immense *Handelstaat*, where the laws of economics are forcing people into misery and disintegrating every form of communitarian solidarity. [. . .] when a nation has conquered the commercial

hegemony, other nations are forced to undermine it, in order to restore a balance: if they can't do so at the expense of the dominant nation, they will inevitably turn their efforts toward the weakest ones. This context of unlimited potential for conflict, generated by the *auri sacra fames*, leads every nation to relentlessly try to expand itself beyond its borders, in order to become an economic power: in this process, all nations are potential losers, and especially the most vulnerable ones. / As suggested by David Harvey, globalization is the flexible and postmodern form of imperialism, i.e. the exact opposite of the soothing and irenic universalism of human rights, as it is presented by the politically correct *pensée unique*.[5]

In short, the target of Fichte's ferocious critique is "Handelsanarchie," where the state just serves the market and guarantees its conditions. Fichte's critique is not based on a particular political opinion but is directly based on his basic philosophical opposition between idealism and dogmatism. The freedom we have in the liberal anarchy of commerce is the freedom to act egotistically (determined by our nature) in a world of exchange that appears as an objective order on which we depend. What is needed is a re-politicization of economy: economic life should be controlled and regulated by the

5. Diego Fusaro, "The Concept of "Commercial Anarchy" in Fichte's *The Closed Commercial State*," https://www.ips.ac.rs/wp-content/uploads/2018/03/Diego-Fusaro_SPT_2_2014.pdf

free decisions of a community, not left to the blind, chaotic interaction of market forces. To paraphrase Kant, Fichte wants to awaken us also from the dogmatic slumber of social life in which our freedom is constrained by objective market mechanisms. Fichte saw clearly that liberal freedom breeds inequality, the non-freedom of the majority, and also brutal competition and colonialism in international relations.

We may not agree with Fichte's proposed measures, but his view of the underlying problem is pertinent—just recall the latest bad surprise from big capital: "Governments around the world—including the UK—face a wave of lawsuits from foreign companies who complain that their profits have been hit by the pandemic."[6] In short, the state (i.e., taxpayers) is expected to compensate corporations for their lost profits as a result of Covid-19 lowering profit rates, as the state is held responsible for guaranteeing the conditions for a stable rate of accumulation. If these lawsuits are pursued, they will be only a logical extension of the ISDS (investor–state dispute settlements) treaties that have been around for decades and that allow companies to sue governments when they implement policies that negatively affect their investments (Swedish company Vattenfall prosecuted Germany for this reason). Today, the state is potentially responsible even if profits are lost due to a health catastrophe,

6. https://www.theguardian.com/law/2020/aug/15/global-law-firms-expected-to-sue-uk-for-coronavirus-losses

(NO TIME) TO CONCLUDE

which has nothing to do with state politics. If our states do not brutally intervene against this, it will be a clear sign that the worst capitalist barbarism is returning.

However, the pressures are not just socio-economic: there are signs that we are simply resigning ourselves to Covid-19. On August 1, 2020, up to 20,000 people marched in Berlin to protest against Germany's coronavirus regulations. The participants included libertarians and anti-vaccination activists, old hippies and new Right populists—as some commentators put it, a mixture of "reggae and Pegida" (Pegida being an extreme right anti-immigrant party). Many flouted guidance on wearing masks and social distancing as they accused the government of "stealing our freedom"; they held up homemade signs with slogans like "Corona, false alarm," "We are being forced to wear a muzzle," "Natural defense instead of vaccination," and "We are the second wave." One of the claims was that the only true conspiracy theory is that there is a pandemic. One of the speakers quoted Saint-Exupéry's *The Little Prince*: "One sees clearly only with the heart."[7] Here, "heart" stands for ideology at its purest— the deeply ingrained, almost "instinctual" stances we assume in daily life. As *Tagesspiegel* reported, "The virus demonstrates that the separation between individuals is no less fictional than the separation between body and world. We 'step into' the world

7. See https://time.com/5874597/coronavirus-restrictions-protest-berlin/

with our feet, we 'grasp' it with our hands, we 'talk about' it with our mouths. This is why the right way to deal with the virus is necessarily unnatural."[8] We encounter here the old gap between science and our everyday life experience, but now brought to the extreme.

The title of Nicol A. Barria-Asenjo's short book on Covid-19, *Construction of a New Normality* (2021), should be taken as seriously as possible. The Covid-19 pandemic shattered not only our healthcare, economy, political and social relations, and mental health, it did something much more radical to which only philosophy can give access: it threatened our sense of "normality," a term we must interpret in all its weight. "Normality" stands for what Lacan called "the big Other": the symbolic order, a network of rules and practices that structures not only our psychic lives but also the way we relate to what we experience as "reality." Here we should take the lesson of the transcendental idea that (what we experience as) reality is not simply "out there," waiting to be discovered, but is mediated ("constituted") by our symbolic universe. An elementary example: in late medieval Europe, "reality" was experienced as permeated by spiritual powers, with even natural phenomena perceived as bearers of hidden meaning, and the cosmos itself as a living Whole controlled by a supreme intelligence. With modernity, meaning

8. https://interaktiv.tagesspiegel.de/lab/karte-sars-cov-2-in-deutschland-landkreise/

is subjectivized, "objective reality" is a mechanism following natural laws, and it is only we humans who project meaning onto it. In his *History of Madness*, Foucault describes another aspect of this shift: the changed status of madness. Even in the Renaissance, madness was considered to be spiritual (a result of possession by sacred or evil spirits), something to be investigated for its secret meaning. With rationalist classicism, madness became a physiological process similar to other illnesses, to be treated in a purely medical way (which is why psychiatric clinics came into being). In his *The Order of Things*, Foucault describes the later shift from classicist systematic rationalism to humanist evolutionism and historicism (encompassing both Darwin and Marx).

These epistemological shifts are not just shifts in our subjective perception of reality, they determine how we conceive and interact with reality. As Georg Lukács put it, nature itself is a historical category, with our basic understanding of what counts as "nature" changing with great historical breaks: in the absolutist seventeenth century, nature appears as a hierarchical system of species and subspecies; in the dynamic nineteenth century, characterized by capitalist competition, nature appears as the site of evolutionary struggle for survival (it is well-known that Darwin invented his theory by way of transposing onto nature Malthus's insights); in the twentieth century, nature was perceived through the lens of systems theory; in recent decades, after the decline of the centralized welfare state, it is a commonplace to draw a parallel between the shift to the auto-poetic, self-organizing dynamic of natural processes and the passage toward new forms of capitalist dynamics.

Why, then, is psychoanalysis needed here, and not just philosophy? It is not only because the Covid-19 pandemic is causing mass-scale mental breakdowns and other psychic pathologies. As Lacan made clear, Freud's basic clinical categories (hysteria, obsessional neurosis, perversion, paranoia) are at the same time transcendental-ontological categories, or what Heidegger called modalities of the disclosure of the world. Obsessional neurosis, for instance, is not just a feature of our psychic lives but is a specific vision of how we relate to reality in its entirety. In the same way, the hysterical question is a mode of doubting our "normality" (defined by the predominant figure of the Master), and paranoia also entails a vision of reality as being dominated by a hidden manipulator who persecutes and controls us.

Barria-Asenjo and Rodrigo Aguilera Hunt recently proposed to interpret the impact of the pandemic by employing the structure of dreams as articulated by Freud.[9] In this, the crucial distinction is one between the content of the dream and

9. Nicol A. Barria-Asenjo and Rodrigo Aguilera Hunt, 'El coronavirus como resto diurno de un sueño traumático en la sociedad chilena', https://www.topia.com.ar/articulos/coronavirus-como-resto-diurno-un-sueno-traumatico-sociedad-chilena

the unconscious wish that it articulates: it is the very cyphering (obfuscation) of the dream content (what Freud calls "dream-thoughts"), its translation into the explicit dream texture, that engenders the properly unconscious content of a dream. This implies that the true secret of a dream is not its hidden content (the dream-thoughts), but its very form—in Freud's terms:

> The latent dream-thoughts are the material which the dream-work transforms into the manifest dream. [. . .] the dream-work never restricts itself to translating these thoughts into the archaic or regressive mode of expression that is familiar to you. In addition, it regularly takes possession of something else, which is not part of the latent thoughts of the previous day, but which is the true motive force for the construction of the dream. This indispensable addition is the equally unconscious wish for the fulfilment of which the content of the dream is given its new form. A dream may thus be any sort of thing in so far as you are only taking into account the thoughts it represents—a warning, an intention, a preparation, and so on; but it is always also the fulfillment of an unconscious wish and, if you are considering it as a product of the dream-work, it is only that.[10]

10. Sigmund Freud, *Introductory Lectures on Psychoanalysis* (Harmondsworth: Penguin Books, 1973), pp. 261–62

The key insight deployed by Freud here is the "triangulation" of latent dream-thought, manifest dream-content, and the unconscious wish: this insight limits the scope of—or, rather, directly undermines—the hermeneutic model of interpreting dreams (the path from the manifest dream-content to its hidden meaning, the latent dream-thought). The dream-work is not merely a process of masking the dream's "true message": the dream's true core, its unconscious wish, inscribes itself only through this process of masking, so that the moment we retranslate the dream-content back into the dream-thought expressed in it, we lose the "true motive force" of the dream—in short, it is the process of masking itself that inscribes into the dream its true secret. One should therefore reverse the standard notion of penetrating ever-deeper into the core of the dream: the "deeper" wish is located in the very gap between the latent dream-thought and the manifest dream-content.

Perhaps a parallel with the digital universe would help here: isn't the distinction between the dream's unconscious wish and the (pre-conscious, at best) dream-thoughts quite similar to that between the dark web and the deep web? One only needs a special code to gain access to a deep web site (like the password for an email account). The dark web is more radically inaccessible: one needs special software even to locate a site in the dark web—the sites themselves, not merely the access to them, are secret, such that the dark web is the

(NO TIME) TO CONCLUDE

Unconscious of the digital universe. Similarly, the panoply of antagonisms and crises that forms the background of the Covid-19 pandemic is its deep web, accessible through simple social analysis, while the transcendental-ontological catastrophe triggered by the pandemic is its dark web, a space that most of us are not even aware of.

Another example of the same distinction is that between simple crimes that violate social laws, and crimes committed by the state itself in its activity of fighting crime (like the illegal control and persecution of individuals)—the first type of crime is the deep web of society, while the second is society's dark web, something that is invisible if we rely simply on the opposition between the law and its violation. The examination of what should be called the "social unconscious" compels us to raise the question: is there a necessary strain of criminality (illegality) that pertains to the power of law as such, that is not simply an accidental misstep of the reign of law but, rather, its constitutive moment?

What does this have to do with Covid-19? My hypothesis is that we can easily locate the same Freudian triad beneath the pandemic as a social fact. Covid-19 itself is the "manifest dream text," the focal point of our media, what we all talk (and dream) about—not just an actual phenomenon but an object of fantasy connections, of dreams and fears. The pandemic is, today, a Master-Signifier, or, as Claudio Magris put it, "a tyrant of our thoughts. Like all tyrants, it wants that we don't talk about anything else than itself."[11] This Master-Signifier is overdetermined by a whole series of interconnected real-life facts and processes (today's riders of the apocalypse) that form its "dream content": not only the reality of the health crisis but also the ecological crisis (global warming, the effects of deep sea pollution and mining, etc.); economic crisis (unemployment, threats of widespread hunger); new waves of social unrest bringing many countries to the edge of civil war; international tensions that can easily erupt into war; and, of course, the mental health crisis. In short, the pandemic functioned as a kind of detonator that exploded already existing tensions in our societies.

This is why Alfredo Eidelsztein is right to emphasize the importance of Lacan's axiom "there is no Other of the Other" in seeking to understand the Covid-19 pandemic.[12] Our most elementary experience is one of decentering: we are not masters in our own house, we are at the mercy of a multi-faced Other, a mixture of (sometimes contradictory) determinations—economic, ideological, social, ecological, and biological. The temptation here is to search behind this multi-faceted Other for an

11. https://www.corriere.it/esteri/20_maggio_07/coronavirus-nuovo-muro-noi-c6cf0f94-8fcc-11ea-bb7f-d3d655d2211a.shtml

12. See https://w.eidelszteinalfredo.com.ar/entrevista-realizada-por-nicol-a-barria-asenjo-para-la-revista-punto-de-fuga-seccion-clinica-de-madrid-nucep/

(NO TIME) TO CONCLUDE

"Other of the Other," a higher entity (God, Fate, Nature) that secretly pulls the strings and controls the game. With regard to the pandemic, there is no single cause (capitalism, climate, China, conspiracy) that can entirely explain it. And nor is the pandemic only the result of the contingent over-determination of multiple processes—it cannot simply be reduced to its (multiple) causes. With Covid-19, something new and unexpected emerged, a contingent global shape that, to put it in Hegelese, retroactively posits its presuppositions. In short, the pandemic is something that contemporary systems theory calls an "emergent property": "those properties that are entirely unexpected and include emergent phenomena in materials and emergent behavior in living creatures. They arise from the collaborative functioning of a system, but do not belong to any one part of that system."[13]

It is because of this complex structure that the prism of the pandemic allows other social events to be seen in their true dimension. Angela Nagle provided a wonderful example in her article, "Will Ireland Survive the Woke Wave?," which notes that many of the intellectuals who protest against racism are often blind—not in the sense that they don't see their own racism, but in the sense that they perceive themselves as members of a "guilty," privileged white elite, instead of as the exploited

13. Quoted from https://sciencing.com/emergent-properties-8232868.html

precarious workers they often are.[14] This is the inverse of the usual problem wherein members of the academic elite play at being in solidarity with the poor and exploited—in the anti-racist protests of today, exploited intellectual workers are engaging in additional self-flagellation. What a wonderful achievement of ideology! California tech giants are leading the struggle against racism and sexism while their actual victims are seduced into practicing self-critical rituals, denigrating their identity. These same tech giants, of course, are those profiting the most from the pandemic.

This is why Duane Rousselle is right to problematize the commonplace claim that, with the pandemic, "everything has suddenly changed"—"everything has suddenly changed only because (and here is my Hegelian moment) things are more the same now than they ever were before."[15] How, exactly, should this be read? The fact that things are now more the same than they have ever been implies that the gap between reality and appearance is an immanent part of reality itself and constitutive of it. To put it bluntly: if we subtract appearance from reality, reality itself disintegrates. To return to the relationship between social reality and ideology, it is too simple to say that beneath the false appearance of freedom and equality there is the reality

14. Angela Nagle, 'Will Ireland Survive the Woke Wave?', https://unherd.com/2020/07/will-ireland-survive-the-woke-wave/

15. All quotes are from private communication with Rousselle.

of racism, sexism and so on—for there is more truth in appearance than in what is beneath it. For Marx, capitalist exploitation does not occur beneath the plane of surface appearances, but is inscribed into the appearance itself (for instance, the appearance of the "free and equal" exchange between capitalist and worker). Racism and sexism are not the hidden cause or truth of exploitation, but can even serve as a fantasmatic mystification of it—for instance, when we attribute exploitation to the subordination of women or Black people, as if racism or the subordination of women is the cause of exploitation. In terms of the pandemic, it is here that I find Rousselle's line of thought ambiguous and insufficient: "We wake up, claimed Lacan, only so that we can continue dreaming in real life. In the same way, isn't it true that the 'alarm clock' function of the pandemic served precisely to wake us up to our deepest pathological behaviors? Does this not explain the rise of xenophobia, racism, domestic abuse, and so on?"

There is a middle term missing in this account: before the pandemic, we were "dreaming in real life" of global capitalist ideology, and in reaction to the pandemic we again awakened (escaped) into ideological reality—but in between the two there was a genuine traumatic break. Let's elaborate this point: how, exactly, does awakening from an ideological dream work? Ideological dreams are not simply opposed to reality—they structure (what we experience as) reality. If, however, what we experience as reality is structured by fantasy, and if fantasy serves as the screen that protects us from being directly overwhelmed by the raw Real, then *reality itself can function as an escape from encountering the Real*. In the opposition between dream and reality, fantasy is on the side of reality, and it is in dreams that we encounter the traumatic Real; thus, it is not that dreams are for those who cannot endure reality, but that reality is for those who cannot endure (the Real that announces itself in) dreams. This is the lesson Lacan draws from the famous dream reported by Freud in his *Interpretation of Dreams*—that of the father who falls asleep while keeping watch over his son's coffin. In this dream, the father's dead son appears to him with a terrible appeal: "Father, can't you see that I am burning?" When the father awakens, he discovers that the cloth on the son's coffin has caught fire due to a candle falling over. Why did the father awaken? Was it because the smell of smoke became too overpowering, so that it was no longer possible for him to prolong his sleep by way of including it into the improvised dream? Lacan proposes a much more interesting reading: it was not the intrusion of the signal from external reality that awakened the unfortunate father, but the unbearably traumatic character of what he encountered in the dream—insofar as "dreaming" means fantasizing in order to avoid confronting the Real, the father literally awakened so that he could go on dreaming. The scenario was as follows: when his sleep was disturbed by the smoke, the father quickly constructed a dream that incorporated the disturbing element

(NO TIME) TO CONCLUDE

(fire) in order to prolong his sleep; however, what he confronted in the dream was a trauma (of responsibility for his son's death) much stronger than reality, so he awakened into reality in order to avoid the Real.

How does this structure work in the case of the Covid-19 pandemic? I rely here again on Barria-Asenjo and Hunt: more fundamentally than the manifest "dream text," the pandemic functions like the intruder from external reality (the equivalent of the burning cloth and its smoke) that disturbs our smooth ideological sleep. This external intruder not only perturbs our daily life but also triggers a traumatic awareness of our global crisis (the equivalent of the appearance of the burning son): "Can't you see that the pandemic is just the tip of the iceberg, a stand-in for a whole series of catastrophes that threaten our very survival, from other forthcoming epidemics to global warming? Can't you see that the pandemic is just a dress rehearsal for a global state of emergency? Can't you see that our world is burning?" This nightmarish vision brings us close to the true awakening, and it is in order to avoid it, i.e., by continuing to dream, that we awaken to ordinary reality. This false awakening has multiple forms: a return to normality (outright denial that Covid-19 is a real threat), conspiracy theories, racism (blaming an ethnic Other for the outbreak), *and* the "New Deal" proposed by the techno-digital wing of corporate capital. This "New Deal" may be resolutely pro-feminist, anti-racist, and so on, but it is still an escape from the real awakening.

Rousselle is right to point out that "Covid-19 wakes us up to 'social distancing' but it does not, in and of itself, introduce it." He explains,

> We go on physically distancing so as to make ourselves believe that the social relationship did in fact once exist (in some prior historical moment before the pandemic); yet, it is clear, from decades of clinical material, that the social relationship never existed. . . . Isn't it the case that during the time of Covid-19—which just so happens to be the time of the McLuhanian "global village"—we are in fact much more socially connected than we have been in the past? For many people— teachers, health workers, and even those who are forced inside small homes with their families—we feel *more* socially connected than ever before. We require new modes of separating from these intensified bonds for our own mental health and well-being.

I read Rousselle's claim that "we go on physically distancing so as to make ourselves believe that the social relationship did in fact once exist (in some prior historical moment before the pandemic)" precisely as an implicit critique of Giorgio Agamben and all those who see in our obeying of quarantine and distancing measures an ethical catastrophe, a willing abandonment of social relationships that once previously existed. As argued earlier, it is the physical distancing implemented in defense against the pandemic that led to intensified social connectivity, not only within quarantined families but also with others outside of them (mostly through digital media), and then triggered outbursts of physical closeness (such as raving and partying). What we've seen with the pandemic was thus not a simple shift from a communal life to a distanced one, but a more complex shift from one constellation of closeness and distancing to another: the fragile balance between communal life and the private sphere characteristic of pre-pandemic society is replaced by a new constellation in which the diminishing of space for actual/ bodily social interaction (due to quarantines, etc.) doesn't lead to more privacy but gives rise to new norms of social dependency and control.

This new constellation comes with many unexpected paradoxes. For example, as Darian Leader noted, state-imposed bodily distancing in a sense makes things easier for us—questions of "How close do I want others to come? How can I create the right distance from others? How can I get others to respect my personal space?" are no longer an inner struggle—the rules are clearly imposed from outside.[16]

> The external imposition of very literal and concrete rules for observing distance helps create and strengthen the boundaries that many people experience as missing in their lives. Now that distancing

16. http://www.journal-psychoanalysis.eu/some-thoughts-on-the-pandemic/

rules are being weakened or abandoned in some parts of the world, we could expect an increase in efforts to re-establish the right distance—which may take, in some cases, violent forms.

I would only add that violence is mostly generated not directly by people's efforts to re-establish the right distance, but as an act of resistance *against* these efforts—recall the numerous reports from around the world about plane and bus passengers reacting violently when asked to wear a mask.

This weird resistance cannot be accounted for by the interplay between the Covid-19 pandemic and the social causes that over-determine it: there is a third level at work here (which vaguely corresponds to the true trauma, the "unconscious wish" of a dream), and this is the ontological catastrophe triggered by the pandemic, the undermining of the coordinates of our basic access to reality that reaches far beyond a usual "mental crisis." This ontological catastrophe also underlies the ongoing massive resurgence of a will not-to-know.

It may appear that, in a time like the present when a virus threatens our lives, our predominant stance would be that of a "will to know": to understand fully the workings of the virus in order to successfully control and eliminate it. However, what we can increasingly witness is a version of the will NOT to know too much about it, insofar as this knowledge could limit our usual way of life. A similar stance was, for a long time, adopted by the Catholic Church, which in response to the rise of modern science, insisted that it was better for us not to know some things. We find an echo of this position even in Kant, the great partisan of Enlightenment, who wrote (in the preface to the second edition of the *Critique of Pure Reason*) that he had to "abolish knowledge in order to make space for belief"—only belief could save our freedom and moral autonomy.[17] Today's cognitive sciences give rise to the same dilemma: if brain science imposes the conclusion that there is no free will, what does this do to our moral autonomy? Since the results of science pose a threat to our (predominant notion of) autonomy and freedom, should we curtail science? The price we pay for the solution to this quandary is a fetishistic split between science and ethics ("I know very well what science claims, but, nonetheless, in order to retain (the appearance of) my autonomy, I choose to ignore it and act as if I don't.") There is a supreme irony in the fact that Habermas, *the* contemporary philosopher of Enlightenment, co-wrote a book with Cardinal Joseph Ratzinger (who later became the conservative Pope Benedict XVI) about the dialectic of secularization in which, in spite of their differences, they both endorse the thesis that human beings inhabit a "post-secular" era in which it becomes clear that the claims of science should be limited so as not to pose a threat to human freedom and

17. https://www.gutenberg.org/files/4280/4280-h/4280-h.htm#chap02

dignity.[18] And those who ignore the true scope of the Covid-19 pandemic act in a similar way: since detailed knowledge about the virus could lead to measures that threaten our idea of a free and dignified life, it is better to act as if nothing serious is occurring—let the scientists search for a vaccine but otherwise leave us alone to continue with life as usual.

To reiterate, I am interested here in what I see as a specific case of the will not-to-know; namely, a widespread refusal to take the pandemic seriously that is now apparent—mostly in the attitudes of new Right populists but also in those of some Leftists—in various forms including outright denial and conspiracy theories. There are five crucial points I want to emphasize here:

(1) What interests me is that, in most of the forms of refusal to *think* Covid-19, ignorance assumes the positive form of a special insider-knowledge, of an insight into what "most people" don't see. Those who deny the seriousness of the pandemic talk about secret conspiracies, a "deep state" plot to impose total social control, etc. In short, ignorance mostly takes the form of an excess-knowledge accessible only to the initiated. (That's why, incidentally, I would never use the image of the three

18. See Jürgen Habermas and Joseph Ratzinger, *Dialektik der Säkularisierung* (Freiburg: Herder Verlag, 2011).

monkeys who see, hear, and say nothing to illus-
trate the prevailing form of ignorance: those with a
will not-to-know have their eyes wide open (seeing
pseudo-facts invisible to others) and listen carefully
(to conspiracy theories.))

(2) One of the prevalent forms of defense against
knowledge of Covid-19 is not direct denial but what
psychoanalysis understands as a fetishistic disavowal that follows the formula "I know very well
(that the pandemic is serious), but"—but I cannot
accept it, I suspend the symbolic efficiency of my
knowledge and continue to act as though I don't
know it. (A similar thing often happens when I
learn that someone close to me has died: rationally
I know it, but I don't really subjectively assume this
knowledge.)

(3) Although I think science is one of our few hopes
today, I don't *simply* trust science—and not only
because scientists can be corrupted by Big Pharma
(and other) companies. There are at least two other
points to be made here: (1) science itself is not uni-
fied, and there are differing theories about Covid-19
that are not the result of economic and political corruption; (2) there are immanent limitations in scientific procedure as such (here referring to modern

positivist natural science), which is why Heidegger wrote that "science doesn't think." To "think" entails here a reflexive procedure that brings ourselves into the picture, and this is not what science does—science cannot fully reflect upon its own social and ideological presuppositions and implications.

(4) This brings me to the next point, which is that I am also fully aware of the positive aspects of ignorance—as Heidegger further points out, the very fact that science doesn't think is its strength. Hegel made a similar point when he praised abstraction as the absolute power of Spirit: to grasp the essence of a phenomenon, one has to erase from the picture, or abstract from, many things. To function in our daily lives, we have to ignore many things, and this holds even for ethics. When someone who's committed a great crime tries to justify or relativize it by explaining how he experienced his act—what was, for him, the deeper meaning—we should a priori dismiss this. It is important to note that behind every ethnic cleansing there is always some "deep" poetic or religious vision. So when a criminal says "try to understand me," the answer is: "No, because the way you interpret the horror you inflicted is a lie you are telling yourself in order to be able to live with it—not the 'inner truth' of it." However, this

general insight has nothing to do with the present efforts to discredit science in the time of Covid-19: there is no positive emancipatory potential in the rage of those who protest against the obligation to wear masks.

(5) The last and perhaps most important point, today and in general, is that the prevalence of the will not-to-know cannot be reduced to the manipulation and constraint of the knowledge of the oppressed by those in power. Two things disturb this image. First, manipulators are also always manipulated in their own way—those in power *also* don't know and can only reign in this way—that's the point of Marx's notion of ideology. Second, the ignorance of the oppressed is not simply imposed on them from outside, but is immanent to their way of life. Let's take the thousands who protest against masks and social distancing from the US to Germany: they act (often violently) because they perceive their freedom and dignity to be threatened. In Slovenia, many parents protested against their children wearing masks in schools saying: "Our children are not dogs who should wear a muzzle in public!" One can understand them: the pandemic has undermined our ingrained sense of "normality"— some of the basic customs that define our way of

life—compelling us to live in ways that we experience as "unnatural." People "ignore" the full truth of the pandemic not because of some epistemological limitation or animalistic will not-to-know, but because of a deep existential anxiety: are we still human when we are forced to act like this?

This is the choice we all have to make: will we succumb to the temptation of the will-to-ignorance or are we ready to really *think* the pandemic, not only as a bio-chemical health issue but as something rooted in the complex totality of our (humanity's) place in nature and of our social and ideological relations—a decision that may entail that we behave "unnaturally" and construct a *new* normality?

APPENDIX: FOUR REFLECTIONS ON POWER, APPEARANCE, AND OBSCENITY

The ongoing pandemic is not only a link in a long chain of crises that besets our world, from threats to our environment to economic and social conflicts; one should also take into account that it exploded in a world characterized by the rise of new populist politics. The interaction between the two—will the pandemic give a new boost to racist, anti-immigrant populism, or will it disclose its inefficiency to a broader public?—as well as the specific nature of the new populism with its open resort to obscenity, deserve a closer examination.

The New Obscene Master

The obscene public space that is emerging today changes the way the opposition between appearance and rumor works. It is not that appearances no longer matter since obscenity reigns directly; it is rather that spreading obscene rumors or acting obscenely paradoxically sustains the appearance of power. In a way, the situation resembles what has happened with the figure of the detective in crime fiction in recent decades: he or she can be crippled, half-crazy or whatever, but his/her authority as the infallible detective remains untouched. In the same way, a political leader can act in undignified ways, make obscene gestures and so on, but all this only strengthens his position as a master. It is similar with Trump who continually surprises us with how far he is willing to go with his vulgar obscenities. As a climax of Trump's attacks on the ex-FBI lawyer Lisa Page, at a Minneapolis rally in October 2019 he performed a mock re-en-actment of text messages she exchanged with Peter Strzok, her ex-lover, as though the couple were in the middle of a sexual act, imitating her orgasmic throes.[1] Lisa Page understandably exploded with rage—but the same story seems to repeat itself: Trump survives yet again what his enemies consider to be the final straw that should destroy him.

We encounter here a new variation on the old motif of the emperor's new clothes: while in the original (Andersen's) version, an innocent child's gaze is needed to publicly proclaim that the emperor is naked, with the reign of public obscenity, the emperor himself proudly proclaims he has no clothes, but this very openness functions as a redoubled mystification—how? In homology with the good old Kantorowicz thesis on the king's two bodies, today's populist emperor has two sets of clothes, so that while he boasts that he is divested of his personal "clothes" of dignity, he retains his second set of clothes, the instruments of his symbolic investiture. For this reason, what makes Trump's obscenity perverse is that not only does he lie brazenly, without any restraint, he also directly tells the truth when one would expect him to be embarrassed by it. When, in August 2020, he announced his intention to defund the US Postal Service, there

1. See https://www.bbc.com/news/world-us-canada-50634645

was no need for a complex analysis to reveal his underlying motivations: when asked why he had decided to defund the post, Trump openly said that it was in order to get less people voting for the Democrats.[2] Lying implies that you still recognize implicitly some moral norms (you just violate them in reality) but what happens with Trump in the described case is worse than lying: in saying what is literally true, he undoes (suspends) the very dimension of truth.

This suspension of the very dimension of truth is clearly apparent in the way Trump dealt with QAnon, a far-right conspiracy theory group alleging a secret plot by a supposed "deep state" against Trump and his supporters. The theory began with an October 2017 post on the anonymous image-board 4chan by "Q," presumably an American individual who was then joined by others. Q claimed to have access to classified information involving the Trump administration and its opponents in the United States. Q has accused many liberal Hollywood actors, Democratic politicians, and high-ranking officials of being members of an international child sex trafficking ring. Q also claimed that Trump feigned collusion with Russians to enlist Robert Mueller to join him in exposing the ring and preventing a coup d'état by Barack Obama, Hillary Clinton, and George Soros. It is interesting to note here

2. See https://www.theguardian.com/us-news/2020/aug/13/
donald-trump-usps-post-office-election-funding

Trump's reaction to QAnon, as reported by ABC news: "The White House on Thursday defended President Donald Trump's embrace of a fringe conspiracy group, with press secretary Kayleigh McEnany saying that he was 'talking about his supporters' when he called QAnon followers people who 'love the country' and said he appreciates their backing."[3] Trump was careful not to say that he takes the QAnon theory seriously, limiting himself to establishing two facts that are, in this case, true: those who advocate QAnon theories are his (Trump's) supporters and they love America. He also added a subjective fact (also true): that he appreciates their backing. This is Trump at his purest: the question of factual truth doesn't even enter the picture. We are thus gradually entering what can be called a post-truth discursive space, a space that oscillates between premodern superstition (conspiracy theories) and postmodern cynical skepticism. Weird incidents like the ones that took place in France in August 2020—"Horses slashed and ears cut off in macabre attacks across France. About 30 incidents have been reported in stables and equine clubs in suspected ritual mutilations"[4]—are also to be counted as part of the general regression from modern rationality (which is needed today more than ever).

3. https://abcnews.go.com/Politics/wh-defends-trumps-embrace-baseless-qanon-conspiracy-followers/story?id=72495721
4. https://www.theguardian.com/world/2020/aug/29/horses-slashed-and-ears-cut-off-in-macabre-attacks-across-france

APPENDIX: FOUR REFLECTIONS ON POWER

The obscene political figures of today are quite opposite to the Stalinist figure of the Leader who is to be kept unblemished at any price. While the Stalinist leader fears that even a minor indecency or imperfection would destroy his position, our new leaders are willing to go quite far in renouncing their dignity—their wager is that this renunciation will work somewhat like the short biographical note on the back of a famous author's book, which is intended to demonstrate that the author, too, is an ordinary human being just like us ("in his free time, X likes collecting butterflies"). Far from undermining the greatness of the author, such a note strengthens this through contrast ("you see? even a great man like X has ridiculous hobbies"). And we are fascinated by the bio note only because he or she is a great author—if it were about an ordinary person, we would be indifferent ("who cares what a nobody like him is doing in his free time?"). The difference between traditional populist leaders and those of today is nonetheless that today's leaders are like the Kim Kardashians of politics: we are fascinated by her because she is famous, but she is famous just for being famous, she doesn't do anything significant. In a similar way, Trump is famous not in spite of his obscenities but on account of them. In the old royal courts, kings often had a clown whose function was to destroy the noble appearance with sarcastic jokes and dirty remarks (thereby confirming by contrast the king's dignity). Trump doesn't need a clown, he is his own clown, and no wonder that his acts are often more funny and tasteless than the performances of his comic imitators. The standard situation is thus inverted: Trump is not a dignified person about whom obscene rumors circulate; he is an (openly) obscene person who wants his obscenity to appear as a mask of his dignity. Alenka Zupančič elaborated the contrast between this logic and the classic logic of domination in which "the smear of the king's image is simultaneously the smear of the king himself and as such inadmissible. The new logic is: let the image be castrated in all possible ways while I can do more or less everything I want. Even more, I can do what I want precisely because of and with the help of this new image."[5]

This, again, is how Trump functions: his public image is smeared in all possible ways, people are surprised at how he continually manages to shock them by reaching a new depth of obscenity, but at the same time he governs in the full sense of the term, imposing unprecedented presidential decrees, etc.— castration is here turned around in an exceptional way. The basic fact of what Lacan calls "symbolic castration" is the gap that separates me—my (ultimately miserable) psychic and social reality—from my symbolic mandate (identity): I am a king not because of my immanent features but because I occupy a certain place in the socio-symbolic edifice, i.e., because others treat me like a king. With today's obscene master, "castration" is displaced onto his public image—Trump makes fun of himself and

5. Quoted from unpublished manuscript.

deprives himself of almost the last vestiges of dignity, he mocks his opponents with shocking vulgarity, but this self-deprecation not only in no way affects the efficiency of his administrative acts, it even allows him to perform these acts with the utmost brutality, as if the open embracing of the "castration" of the public image (renouncing the insignia of dignity) enables the full "non-castrated" display of actual political power. It is crucial to grasp that the "castration" of the public image is not simply a signal that this image does not matter and that it is only actual administrative power that counts; rather, the full deployment of administrative power, of enforcing measures, is only possible when the public image is "castrated."

But what about a politician who both acts like an efficient, no-nonsense administrator and also publicly assumes such an image ("a matter-of-fact guy who despises empty rituals and is only interested in results")? The gap between the public image and the actual person is still at work in such an identity, and one can easily detect the difference between a truly efficient administrator and a person who only adopts the appearance of one. But more important is the fact that assuming the image of the efficient administrator seriously constrains the limits of what I am able to do in reality, of how I can exercise my power: I have to obey certain rules. Why, then, do today's populist leaders renounce the dignity of their official position in order to exercise full power? Trump's exercise of presidential power involves not just two but three elements: his ruthless exercise of power (enforcing decrees), his clownish-obscene public image, AND the symbolic site of power—although this site is emptied of its positive content (dignity), it remains fully operative, and it is precisely its emptiness that enables Trump to fully exercise his administrative power.

Trump is often perceived as somebody who spreads obscene rumors—but is this the case? Rumors are a specific mode of the big Other, they are in some sense the other side, the obverse, of the big Other that stands for the dignity of public space.[6] Recall the typical situation of a small group of people who all know some embarrassing secret about one of their number, and they all know that every one of them knows that they all know it—but nonetheless a radical break occurs when one of them says it out loud. Nobody learned anything new— why, then, does it cause such embarrassment? Because they can no longer pretend (act as if) they don't know it—now the big Other knows it. This is the big Other of appearances, and the domain of rumors is precisely its opposite. However, rumors do not convey the factual truth hidden behind appearances: in spite of their opposition, rumors and appearances are both outside factual truth. To save the appearance of dignity we are ready to keep silent on truth, but the anonymous rumors excluded from the public space also remain efficient even if not true—usually

6. I rely here on Mladen Dolar who elaborated the concept of rumor in all its dimensions.

taking the form of "I don't know if this is really true, but I was told (or, rather, the impersonal 'one says that') X did this and that." A blistering case of rumors spread in the form of disavowal was provided by one of the main Russian national TV networks, Channel One, which launched a regular slot devoted to coronavirus conspiracy theories on its main evening news program, Vremya ("Time"). The reporting style is ambiguous, appearing to debunk the theories while leaving viewers with the impression that they contain a kernel of truth. The message (shadowy Western elites and especially the US are somehow ultimately to blame for the pandemic) is thus propagated as a doubtful rumor: it's too crazy to be true, but then again, who knows?[7] The suspension of actual truth strangely doesn't annihilate its symbolic efficiency. Rumors and appearance thus both maintain a distance from factual truth—sometimes, our respect for another's dignity even demands us to publicly declare something that we ourselves—as well as those we address—know to be factually untrue.

But doesn't such an openly obscene suspension of truth undermine the very foundations of rational critique, rendering it inoperative? Does it not present an insurmountable obstacle to the idea that there may be some progressive potentials in the crisis triggered by the pandemic? Jacqueline Rose made a similar critical point against me (during a Birkbeck Summer School

7. https://www.bbc.com/news/world-europe-51413870

debate): "How do you square the release of obscenity, even psychosis, into public political space and your account of the progressive elements of the moment? Can ethics defeat obscenity—I fear that the whole of psychoanalysis suggests not." I think things are more complex. Perverse obscenity is not the moment when the unconscious erupts into the open without any ethical regulations to constrain it. Freud wrote that in perversion, the unconscious is most difficult to access, which is why it is almost impossible to psychoanalyze perverts—first they have to be hystericized, their assurances weakened by the rise of hysterical questions. But I think that what we are witnessing now, with the pandemic just dragging on, is just such a gradual hystericization of those who assumed perverse or even psychotic positions. Trump and other new Right populists are breaking down, getting nervous, their reactions becoming increasingly inconsistent, self-contradictory, and haunted by questions. To return to Rose: I think that obscenity itself already relies on a certain ethics, it assumes a certain stance that cannot but be designated as ethical—those who act obscenely want to shock people with their acts and, in this way, awaken them from their everyday illusions. The way to overcome this ethics of obscenity is to reveal its inconsistencies: those who act obscenely have their own taboos, they are never as radical as they think they are. There is no politician today more constrained by the repression of his unconscious than Trump—precisely when he pretends to act and speak with sincerity and openness, saying whatever comes to his mind.

Oppression, Repression, Depression

Let us recapitulate the results of the above. Not so long ago, in a galaxy that now appears far, far away, the public space was clearly distinguished from the obscenities of private exchanges. Politicians, journalists, and other media personalities were expected to address us with a minimum of dignity, speaking and acting as if the common good was their main concern, avoiding vulgar expressions and reference to personal intimacies. There were, of course, rumors about their private vices, but they remained just that—private matters mentioned only in the yellow press. Today, however, not only can we read in the mainstream media the intimate details of the lives of public personalities, but populist politicians themselves often regress to shameless obscenity. It is the very *public* domain in which "fake news" circulates and rumors and conspiracy theories abound.

One should not lose sight of what is so surprising about this rise of the shameless obscenity of the alt-right so well analyzed by Angela Nagle in her book *Kill All Normies*.[8] Traditionally (or in our retroactive view of tradition, at least), shameless obscenity worked subversively, as an undermining of traditional domination, as depriving the Master of his false dignity. I remember

8. See Angela Nagle, *Kill All Normies* (New York: Zero Books, 2017).

from my own youth in the 1960s, protesting students liked to use obscene words and gestures to embarrass figures of power and, so they claimed, denounce their hypocrisy. However, what is happening today with the growth of public obscenity is not the disappearance of authority, of Master figures, but its forceful reappearance—we are getting something that was unimaginable decades ago: obscene Masters.

Donald Trump is the emblematic figure of this new type of obscene populist Master, and the usual line of argumentation against him—that his populism (concern for the well-being of ordinary people) is fake, and that his actual politics protect the interests of the rich—is insufficient. The followers of Trump do not act "irrationally," they are not victims of primitive ideological manipulations that make them vote against their interests. They are quite rational in their own terms: they vote for Trump because in the "patriotic" vision he promotes, he also addresses their ordinary, everyday problems—safety, stable employment, etc.

When Trump was elected president, publishers asked me to write a book that would submit the Trump phenomenon to a psychoanalytic critique, and my answer was that we do not need psychoanalysis to explore the "pathology" of Trump's success—the only thing to psychoanalyze is the irrational stupidity of Left liberal reactions to it, the stupidity that makes it increasingly probable that Trump will be reelected. To appropriate what is perhaps the lowest point of Trump's vulgarities, the Left has not yet learned how to grab Trump by his p****.

APPENDIX: FOUR REFLECTIONS ON POWER

Trump is not winning simply by shamelessly bombarding voters with messages that generate obscene enjoyment in how he dares to violate the elementary norms of decency. Through all his shocking vulgarities, he is providing his followers with a narrative that makes sense—a very limited and twisted sense, but nonetheless one that is obviously more effective than the Left-liberal narrative. His shameless obscenities serve as signs of solidarity with so-called ordinary people ("you see? I am the same as you, we are all red under our skin"), and this solidarity also signals the point at which Trump's obscenity reaches its limit. Trump is not thoroughly obscene: when he talks about the greatness of America, when he dismisses his opponents as enemies of the people, etc., he intends to be taken seriously, and his obscenities are meant to emphasize by contrast, the level on which he is serious: they are meant to function as an obscene display of his belief in the greatness of America.

This is why, in order to undermine Trump, one should begin by displacing the site of his obscenity and treat as obscene precisely his "serious" statements. Trump is not truly obscene when he uses vulgar sexist or racist terms, he is truly obscene when he talks about America as the greatest country in the world, or when he imposes his economic measures. The obscenity of his speech masks this more basic obscenity. One could paraphrase here the already-mentioned Marx Brothers dictum: Trump looks and acts like a shamelessly obscene politician, but this should not deceive us—he really is a shamelessly obscene politician.

Public obscenity that proliferates today constitutes a third domain between the private and the public space: the private space elevated into the public sphere. This hybrid domain best fits our immersion into cyberspace, our participation in chatrooms, our tweeting, instagramming, facebooking, Trump, of course, makes most of his decisions public through Twitter, but his posts do not give us the "real Trump": the domain of public obscenities is not that of sharing intimate experiences, it is a public domain full of lies, hypocrisies, and pure malevolence, in which we interact as though we are wearing a disgusting mask. The standard relationship between my intimacy and the big Other of public dignity is thus turned around: obscenities are no longer limited to private exchanges, they explode in the public domain itself, allowing me to dwell in the illusion that it's all just an obscene game while I remain innocent in my intimate purity. The first task of a critic is to demonstrate how this purity is a fake—in all domains, not only in politics but also in entertainment. Let's take a look at the latest example:

> Gwyneth Paltrow has made a strong business out of her vagina. She—through her wellness platform Goop—introduced us to the concept of vaginal steaming, jade vaginal eggs and, of course, the elusive sex dust moon juice. Now, new for January 2020, we have the vagina

candle, which has already sold-out, prompting a waitlist. [. . .] The goal, the Goop description optimistically
reads, is "to put us in mind of fantasy, seduction, and
a sophisticated warmth". If you do manage to buy one
through the waitlist, it'll cost $75 or £58.[9]

Again, Paltrow's implicit point here is that she is just playing an
obscene game while retaining her intimate dignity—and this is
what one should reject: no, her intimate dignity is a false mask
concealing the fact that she is openly merchandising her vagina.[10] And one can easily imagine a consumer protection agency
raising the question: how does the customer know that the
product really smells like Paltrow's vagina? Is there a way to
verify this?

What we encounter here, in such false permissiveness, is
the difference between oppressive repression and permissive
oppression. Referring to Alain Ehrenberg's *The Weariness of the
Self*, Petra Kettl and Robert Pfaller wrote in their article, "The
End of Cinema as We Used to Know It":

9. Quoted from https://www.harpersbazaar.com/uk/beauty/
   fragrance/a30510012/gwyneth-paltrow-vagina-candle/
10. And the trend goes on – singer Erykah Badu announced that
    she will sell vagina incense made from her used underwear
    . . . See https://www.msn.com/en-gb/lifestyle/style/erykah-
    badu-to-sell-vagina-incense-made-from-her-used-underwear/
    ar-BBZIHxr?ocid=spartanntp

Earlier decades, Ehrenberg argues, were marked by "repression" (in the psychoanalytic sense): people wanted many things, but society's strict rules put limits upon them. The subsequent crisis was a crisis of "being allowed to." Today's society, on the contrary, is a society of "depression." Society has become permissive in many respects and allows for a couple of hitherto prohibited or accursed things, but people find themselves unable to desire them. The subsequent crisis is a crisis of longing—the typical problem of melancholia, fatigue, and depression.[11]

Before the postmodern permissive turn, our culture was characterized by the structure of inherent transgression: the law, which prohibited certain acts, secretly called for the transgression of some prohibitions and in this way kept our desire alive. Today, nothing (no sexual activity) is clearly prohibited, but the very coordinates of our desire are, consequently, lost. Why? What should be avoided here is the apparently "logical" conclusion that we need prohibition to sustain desire, that desires thrive on the prohibitions they are transgressing. Along these lines, toward the end of his life Georges Bataille spoke against the sexual revolution of the 1960s: if everything is permitted, then desire is killed. But a return to repression is not the answer to depression—not even in a mild form of imagining a Master

11. https://crisiscritique.org/2020/july/petra&robert.pdf

who would sustain prohibitions (not in a strict or brutal way, but only enough to keep our desire for transgression alive)—we cannot cheat in this way. The secret of why permissiveness kills desire lies elsewhere—let's again take a brief look at Political Correctness, which purports to guarantee to everybody the expression of desire but is actually more oppressive than traditional repression. A very strong desire survives in the PC stance: the desire to discover guilt, to suspect racist and sexist evil everywhere and to annihilate it. This desire is sustained by a thick network of rules whose violation is *really prohibited*: no dirty jokes, no sexual "harassment,"

In his novel *Another Now*, Yanis Varoufakis applies the opposition between repression and depression to social reality itself.[12] The plot in brief is that a group of individuals in our capitalist present find a way to communicate with and then enter an alternate reality ("Another Now") in which, following the 2008 crisis, history took a different turn, and the result is a global society of democratic market socialism: there is one central state bank that regulates the money supply in a transparent way, financial speculation disappears because it becomes meaningless, ownership is dispersed since each citizen is allocated their part, healthcare and human rights are guaranteed for everyone, etc.—in short, it's a self-managed global society

12. See Yanis Varoufakis, *Another Now: Dispatches from an Alternative Present* (London: The Bodley Head, 2020). Numbers in brackets refer to the pages of this book.

in which every particular demand finds a way to be heard, so
there are no antagonisms and no reasons to rebel. The choice
our group confronts is: should they remain in Another Now or
return to our neoliberal Now with all of its struggles and violence? Varoufakis gives a series of features that spoil the perfec-
tion of Another Now. First, although economic alienation and
exploitation are overcome, and the state as an alienated entity
is dissolved in the transparent self-management of the society,
the repression of women subtly survives at the level of everyday
practices. (Here I disagree with Varoufakis: I think that today we
also face the opposite possibility: a postmodern multicultural
society in which racism and patriarchy are left behind but economic exploitation remains.) Second, market exchange and the
competitive stance that it implies remain in full force:

> I am, I admit, fascinated, impressed, awestruck even,
> by what the rebels have achieved in the Other Now,
> particularly the democratization of corporations,
> money, land ownership and markets. Except that
> democratized markets still prioritize the transactional
> quid pro quo mentality that undermines the sover-
> eignty of good and, ultimately, our fundamental well-
> being. Democratized market societies, freed from cap-
> italism, are infinitely preferable to what we have here,
> except for one crucial thing: they entrench exchange
> value and thereby, I fear, make impossible a genuine

revolution that leads to the final toppling of markets. (218–9)

In the terms of the Frankfurt School, something like "instrumental reason" remains in this calculating exchange society: there is no space for simple goodness, for acts done just for the sake of it, out of love, without anything expected in exchange. And one could add that what would have ruined the society imagined in Another Now is envy as constitutive of human desire. For Lacan, the fundamental impasse of human desire is that it is the other's desire in both subjective and objective genitive: desire for the other, desire to be desired by the other, and, especially, desire for what the other desires. Envy and resentment are thus a constitutive component of human desire, as Augustine already knew so well—recall the passage from his *Confessions*, often quoted by Lacan, the scene of a baby who is jealous of his brother sucking at the mother's breast: "I myself have seen and known an infant to be jealous though it could not speak. It became pale, and cast bitter looks on its foster-brother." Aware of this constitutive role of envy, Jean-Pierre Dupuy[13] proposed a convincing critique of Rawls' theory of justice: in Rawls' model of a just society, social inequalities are tolerated only insofar as they also help those at the bottom of the social ladder, and insofar as they are not based on inherited hierarchies but on natural inequalities, which are

13. Jean-Pierre Dupuy, *Avions-nous oublie le mal? Penser la politique après le 11 septembre* (Paris: Bayard, 2002)

considered contingent, not merits.[14] What Rawls doesn't see is
how such a society would create conditions for an uncontrolled
explosion of resentment: in it, I would know that my lower status was fully justified, and would thus be deprived of excusing
my failure as being the result of social injustice. Lacan shares
with Nietzsche and Freud the idea that justice conceived as
equality is founded on envy: envy of the other who has what we
do not, and who enjoys it.

In his *An American Utopia*, Fredric Jameson totally rejects
the predominant optimist view according to which Communism
will leave behind envy as a remainder of capitalist competition,
to be replaced by solidarity, collaboration, and taking pleasure
in others' pleasures. Dismissing this myth, he emphasizes that
in Communism, precisely insofar as society will be more just,
envy and resentment will explode. Why? The demand for justice is ultimately the demand that the excessive enjoyment of
the other be curtailed, so that everyone's access to enjoyment is
made equal. The necessary outcome of this demand, of course,
is ascetism: since it is not possible to impose equal enjoyment,
what *can* be imposed is equally shared *prohibition*. However,
one should not forget that today, in our allegedly permissive
society, this ascetism assumes precisely the form of its opposite, of the generalized injunction "Enjoy!" We are all under the

14. See John Rawls, *A Theory of Justice* (Cambridge, MA: Harvard
University Press, 1971 (revised edition 1999)).

spell of this injunction, with the result that our enjoyment is more hindered than ever. This, perhaps, is what Nietzsche had in mind with his notion of the Last Man—it is only today that we can really discern the contours of the Last Man, in the guise of the prevailing hedonistic asceticism.

Third, due to its very transparency, the society in Another Now is one of total control: my properties and activities are transparent to others, my behavior is regulated in a severe PC way, etc. Fourth, again due to its democratic transparency and justice, there is nothing to rebel against in *Another Now*—this is how Iris, the old radical Leftist character, is described:

> raging against the system was Iris's only way of being, her loneliness vaccine. The Other Now was too pleasant, too wholesome to rage against. It would have made Iris's life intolerable.(219) "Surely if there is one thing you know about me, Yango," she replied cheerfully, "it is that I am a dissident. There was nothing for me on the other side to dissent from except their political correctness and smugness at having created the perfect society."(228) "This Now, my dear Yango, is my natural habitat—it's so bloody awful that I feel alive and usefully dangerous. Having experienced the rebellion and seen the institutions it created, I am more confident over here than anyone I know when lambasting the stupidity of the ruling class and its system. It is far easier to subvert them here, let me tell you!" (229).

Would Iris not feel quite at home in Belarus today (August 2020), where a rebellion against the unpopular tyrant is raging? (The situation is much more obscure in Ukraine where the rebellion has won but the poverty drags on.) The question is, again, how to resolve the deadlock between repression (in our Now) and depression (in Another Now)? And how can we avoid the obvious but false conclusion that, since rebellion is the essence of our lives, in the absence of a force of oppression we must construct one in order to then be able to resist it? Would Iris really accept the needless continual suffering of millions just so she could act and feel like a true rebel? The typical solution is to avoid the deadlock by way of positing that the struggle against oppression is endless, new forms of oppression always arise. This solution was criticized by Hegel in his analysis of the contradictions that inhabit Kant's moralism of infinite task, or, to quote Findlay's concise resume: "If the highest good is taken to be a Nature which conforms to morality, morality itself vanishes from this good, since it presupposes a non-conforming Nature. Moral action, being the absolute purpose, seems to look to the elimination of moral action."[15] Is this not what Iris is complaining about? Rebellion, being the absolute purpose, seems to look to the elimination of rebellion. The only solution to this deadlock is the Hegelian one: we should abandon the very ideal of a self-transparent society wherein full

15. https://www.marxists.org/reference/archive/hegel/help/findlay4.htm

APPENDIX: FOUR REFLECTIONS ON POWER

democracy abolishes all alienated structures. Alienation is a condition of our freedom, it gives us breathing space to exercise freedom. I am free only insofar as the big Other (social substance) in which I dwell is non-transparent to me AND TO ITSELF (there is no secret Master who pulls the strings). Reconciliation means that we have to reconcile ourselves with alienation, not its overcoming, so the problem with Another Now is precisely that it effectively abolishes alienation.

The New Populism Is Not Fascism
Trump's inconsistencies exploded with the Covid-19 pandemic. The confused improvisations in Trump's reaction to the virus outbreak were widely noticed: first he praised China's measures, then he blamed China and the Democrats for America's woes, and all of this mixed with his eccentric claims about possible cures and calls for a fast return to normal. This mixture of obscenities, political paranoia, and folk wisdom perfectly exemplifies the nature of today's new Right populism, but it also shows the difference between traditional "totalitarian" populism and today's new Right populism. So let's use this opportunity to take a step back and analyze more closely the unique nature of today's populism. (I rely here extensively on Yuval Kremnitzer's work.)[16]

16. The uncredited quotes that follow are from Yuval Kremnitzer, "The Emperor's New Nudity: The Media, the Masses, and the Unwritten Law" (manuscript).

Like any populism, today's distrusts political representation, pretending to speak directly for the people—it complains about how its hands are tied by the "deep state" financial establishment, claiming: "if only we didn't have our hands tied, we would be able to do away with our enemies once and for all." However, in contrast to the old authoritarian populism (like Fascism) that is ready to abolish formal representative democracy and completely impose a new order, today's populism doesn't have a coherent vision of some new order—the positive content of its ideology and politics is an inconsistent bricolage of measures aimed at bribing "our own" poor, lowering taxes for the rich, and focusing hatred on immigrants and the corrupt elite that is outsourcing jobs, etc. That's why today's populists don't really want to get rid of the established representative democracy and fully take power: "without the 'fetters' of the liberal order to struggle against, the new right would actually have to take some real action," and this would render obvious the vacuity of their program. That is the first feature of today's populists: they can only function in the indefinite postponement of achieving their goal since their coherence relies on opposing the "deep state" of the liberal establishment: "The new right does not, at least not at this stage, seek to establish a supreme value—for instance, the nation, or the leader—that would fully expresses the will of the people and thereby allow and perhaps even require the abolition of the mechanisms of representation."

APPENDIX: FOUR REFLECTIONS ON POWER

So how do today's populists deal with this immanent antagonism of their project whereby they don't really want to destroy their proclaimed enemy? Here, style replaces the lack of political substance; namely, the style of direct appeal to obscenity that violates (some of) the unwritten rules of a society. Every order of culture implies a specific set of unwritten rules that regulate what one is not allowed to talk about publicly. These unwritten rules operate at multiple levels, from rumors about the dark side of the private lives of political leaders and the use of dirty language and indecent insinuations, to cases that are much more "innocent" and as such even more crucial. Here is an extreme case of the prohibition of publicly stating the obvious— in the last years of his life, Deng Xiaoping officially retired, but everybody knew that he continued to pull the strings of power. When one of the high Chinese party apparatchiks referred to Deng as the de facto leader of China in an interview with a foreign journalist, he was nonetheless accused of publicly disclosing a state secret and severely punished. As is evident here, a state secret is not necessarily something that only a few are allowed to know, but can also be something that everybody knows—everybody except what Lacan calls the big Other, the order of public appearance. Now, obscenity is not co-substantial with unwritten rules, nor is it the result of unwritten rules being made explicit; rather, obscenity emerges when we *violate* the unwritten rules, when we do or say something that, while not explicitly prohibited, we all know shouldn't be done or said. For example—and it is a sad and terrifying example—although one doesn't talk about this a lot, it is clear that not only Brazil but rich countries like the US and Sweden decided to sacrifice thousands of lives to Covid-19, especially those of the old and ill, to maintain the economy and the appearance of normal life. While everyone knows this terrible truth, to state it publicly would be obscene—we find here an unwritten rule that, perhaps, should be respected. A more ridiculous example: everybody knows that flatulence in public is considered extremely tasteless, but to state this rule publicly is in itself an obscene act. (Only Trump has the gall to do so: when he once praised Melania as a refined lady in a public talk, he said that in all their life together he never heard her emit a fart.)

With the new Right populism, something unique happens—it has become possible "for the political, which is supposed to reside on the side of the decent, to drastically switch sides and appeal directly to the obscene [. . .] what makes this new form of authority so challenging to comprehend is the explicit way in which it makes exposure operate perversely as illusion; the act of taking off the mask functions as a mask." Note Kremnitzer's precise formulation: the very gesture of taking off the mask and brutally stating what one means functions as a mask. Why? Because the obscene form masks the vacuity of its content. The function of obscenity is here very precise: it is supposed to be the indicator of "medial sincerity" (as opposed to the liberal insistence on sticking to formal rules). Trump endlessly varies this motif: he admits he is constantly breaking the rules (not just) of politeness, resorting to vulgar insinuations and throwing unverified or even blatantly false accusations at his enemies, but he presents this as a proof that he really means it, in contrast with liberal formal politeness. In a quasi-Marxist way, today's populists denounce a political bias in the very formal procedures of representative politics: the rules of the game aren't really neutral and equal for all participants, they are made to prevent and manipulate the direct adequate expression of the people's will. This is the game today's populists play: while remaining within the "representational logic" of liberal political space, they constantly evoke its lies and try to "bring forward that which eludes the representational logic": the populists' vulgar excesses

> [mark] the polite liberal opposition as one that hypocritically denies that which the right is no longer afraid to parade publicly for all to see. The truth exposed by the right—the revelation that the symbolic order is nothing but a show of sanctimony put on to conceal violent reality—is congruent with the anti-ideological project of critical thinking, and therefore criticism finds itself powerless to oppose it.

In this sense, the populist critique is symmetrically opposed to the Politically Correct disclosure of the illusions of liberal neutrality—they supplement and reinforce each other: "the left's moral outrage feeds the right's appetite for transgression, which feeds the left's moral outrage, and the cycle continues." To understand the fatal failure of the Politically Correct stance, one has to introduce the Lacanian division between pleasure and *jouissance*, its traumatic excess. To put it bluntly, what the PC regulation tries to get rid of is not pleasure but enjoyment in its traumatic dimension, as a mixture of pleasure and pain, desire and violence. The PC stance, of course, accepts masochism, but in a strictly consensual form: I must explicitly agree for you to beat me, or whatever. The implication of this stance is that, at a distance from the mess of my desires, I have a clear rational ego that knows what I really want, and this ego should give you my explicit consent. But what if things get mixed here, what if there is a gray zone in which what I desire cannot be formulated as my consent? What if, say, I want to be beaten and humiliated by you precisely *against* my consent, *without* agreeing to it, so that my explicit consent would ruin everything? And what if *jouissance* dwells precisely in this gray zone?

So let's be more precise here: we have four positions. First, there is the liberal–formal legalism that trusts the neutrality of the procedures of political representation. Then, there are the three critical positions toward this stance. The first of these is the Politically Correct analysis that reads the official liberal neutrality with suspicion and tries to bring out its racial, cultural, and gender biases. The PC stance remains within the basic liberal coordinates, it just wants to fully actualize them by abolishing the hidden biases—the problem is that it focuses on individual responsibility. With moralist zeal, it analyzes the details of the subject's behavior, searching for traces of racism and sexism. But its domain is that of cultural and sexual identity, not of radical economic and social change; it extols you to change your behavior, to get rid of racial and sexist clichés, not to analyze the society that gives birth to them.

The second critical position is that of obscene populism whose shocking power resides in its readiness to openly state what the PC critic is trying to unearth through refined analysis—the obscene populist asserts his innocence by way of admitting in advance (what is, in the eyes of the PC critic) his guilt. This in a way renders the PC analysis useless—it is trying to break through an open door—so no wonder that PC critics spend much of their time analyzing each other, discovering traces of racism and sexism in apparently respectful statements and gestures. Or, as Shuja Haider put it succinctly, "It should go without saying that Left-liberal identity politics and Alt-right white nationalism are not comparable. The problem is that they are compatible."[17]

The PC puritan moralism and the new Right populist display of public obscenity are the two sides of the same

17. Quoted from https://unherd.com/2020/07/will-ireland-survive-the-woke-wave/

coin—neither really does what it promises. The problem with populist obscenity is not that it's morally irresponsible, but that it is not really obscene: the daredevil stance of ignoring rules of decency and unrestrainedly saying whatever comes to one's mind is a fake stance that conceals a thick underworld of unwritten rules that prescribe what one can and cannot say. In a homologous way, it's not that the PC stance is too rigidly moralistic and lacks the liveliness of obscenity—no, PC excessive moralism is a fake stance because it covers up opportunist calculus, hypocrisy, and self-righteousness. It is full of its own unwritten rules: minorities who count more than others; subtly different criteria for what is prohibited and what is allowed that change as quickly as fashion; anti-racism that is based on hidden racist arrogance (a white guy who solicits others to assert their identity renounces his identity and thereby reserves for himself the position of universality); and, especially, the awareness of which questions are NOT to be raised (i.e. that of radical social change). There should be more women in positions of power, but the power structure itself should not change; we should help the poor, but we should remain rich; a position of power at a university should not be abused for sexual favors from those subordinate to us, but power that isn't sexualized is OK. Angela Nagle and Michael Tracey were right to identify the main reason for Sanders's defeat in his struggle for nomination as being the movement of his campaign from an emphasis on popular class insurgency to liberal anti-Trump resistance—from class war to

Culture War.[18] Eager to please the Democratic liberal Left, he increasingly subordinated class insurgency to cultural topics; for instance, he tacitly endorsed the Left liberal view that the main danger is not global capitalism but Trump's "Fascism," against which we should all unite. It is no surprise that Biden is playing this game of anti-Trump unity quite well—there are now rumors that George Bush will support him against Trump.

Biden, who is now supported even by neo-cons, is like Chauncey Gardner from *Being There* (a Hal Ashby movie based on Jerzy Kosiński's short novel), in which Peter Sellers plays the US president's autistic, socially isolated gardener. When the president dies unexpectedly, Sellers is mistaken for the president's wise confidant, and his naïve sayings about how to cultivate a garden are interpreted as encoded insights into how to run international affairs—simply because he "is there." Likewise, simply by "being there" and making little sense, Biden will be an ideal president for corporate-financial capital, allowing it all the freedom it wants.[19] His universally praised speech at the Democratic convention was one big piece of bullshit: unity, empathy, no economy, no social justice. Even Fox News praised it, and no doubt Trump will use this speech as a point of reference to underscore his claim to be protecting ordinary workers

18. See https://americanaffairsjournal.org/2020/05/first-as-tragedy-then-as-farce/
19. I owe this idea to Yanis Varoufakis (private conversation).

from the clutches of big financial institutions. The November 2020 elections will thus again be a displaced and mystified form of the class struggle as expressed in the opposition between Trumpian populism and its enemies, as represented by the mega-corporations.[20]

And the third critical position? It is simply that of the Leftist Achilles—from the paradox of Achilles and the tortoise—who haunts the Politically Correct stance. This paradox is clearly discernible in the open letter published by *Harper's Magazine*, which argued against the excesses of Political Correctness and was signed by two different groups of people: liberals for whom Political Correctness is too radical, and true Leftists for whom it *is not radical enough*. So the PC Achilles never reaches the tortoise of the fully non-racist/sexist society and remains caught in permanent self-questioning: just when he thinks he is rid of racism and sexism, the tortoise moves a little bit farther and there are new, more severe criteria delineating what is racist and sexist. The Leftist Achilles does something else: instead of

20. The forceful return of class struggle in our era doesn't mean that all conflicts can be reduced to it; it means that other big struggles that preoccupy our media are overdetermined by class struggle as its displaced effects. As Matthew Klein and Michael Pettis convincingly demonstrated in their *Trade Wars Are Class Wars* (New Haven: Yale University Press, 2020), the ongoing "trade war" between the US and China can only be understood if one analyzes them against the background of the class struggle in the US and in China.

trying to reach the tortoise (to fully meet the PC criteria), he realizes that these criteria are themselves inherent to capitalist society and overtakes them, moving further in the direction of socio-economic change.

The Crisis of New Populism

In the time of Covid-19, the world order as we knew it is disintegrating. Countries are cutting links with the World Health Organization and other international organizations, and they are revoking old armament agreements. Trump has announced an intention to deploy the army on the streets of US cities, China is discussing a possible military invasion of Taiwan, and Putin has said that Russia may use nuclear arms if it were to be attacked by conventional arms. Along these lines, nationalist populists were expected to seize the opportunity of the Covid-19 pandemic and transform their countries into isolated fiefdoms directed against foreign enemies—but it didn't work, their bravados turned into a blatant display of impotence and incompetence. Let's take the three big authoritarian populists, as Angela Dewan puts it—"Trump, Putin and Bolsonaro find their populist playbooks are no match for coronavirus":

> The coronavirus pandemic could have been a moment of glory for the world's populist leaders. This is a period of heightened fear and anxiety—emotions that typically allow them to thrive. Instead, some populists are finding themselves powerless against the

outbreaks ravaging their countries. The US, Brazil and
Russia now have the highest number of coronavirus
cases in the world, and as their death tolls continue to
rise, their economies are taking devastating blows.[21]

Donald Trump found himself in a special predicament when the
Covid-19 crisis was joined by the nationwide protests against
the killing of George Floyd, beginning in May 2020. Floyd's last
words, "I can't breathe," are also often the last words of a person dying of Covid-19. The link is obvious: a much higher per-
centage of Black people than white people are affected by both
police violence and by the coronavirus. Confronted with this
situation, Trump is simply out of his league: unable to impose a
unifying vision, to perform the gesture of a leader in a situation
that desperately calls for one, or to acknowledge the gravity of
the situation and offer some kind of hope and vision. As Robert
Reich wrote: "You'd be forgiven if you hadn't noticed. His verbal
bombshells are louder than ever, but Donald Trump is no longer
president of the United States."[22] When he threatened that if the
police and National Guard could not impose calm, he would
send in the army to crush the protests with its "infinite force,"
Trump became the agent and instigator of a civil war.

21. https://edition.cnn.com/2020/05/31/world/
coronavirus-trump-bolsonaro-putin-populists-intl/
22. https://www.theguardian.com/commentisfree/2020/
may/31/donald-trump-coronavirus-pandemic-george-floyd-
minneapolis-tweets

APPENDIX: FOUR REFLECTIONS ON POWER

But what, precisely, is this war? One aspect of the ongoing protests in the US that has not been emphasized enough, although it is absolutely crucial, is that there is no place for the dissatisfaction that fuels the protests within the arena of the "Culture War" between the Politically Correct liberal Left and populist neo-conservatives. The liberal Left's stance toward protests is: yes to dignified peaceful protests, but no to extremist destructive excesses and looting. In some elementary sense they are right, of course, but they miss the meaning of violent excesses; namely, that they are a reaction to the fact that the peaceful liberal path of gradual political change hasn't worked, that systemic racism persists in the US. What emerges in violent protests is an anger that cannot be adequately represented in our political space.

This is also why so many representatives of the establishment—not only liberals but also conservatives—are openly critical of Trump's aggressive stance toward the protesters: the establishment desperately wants to channel protests into the coordinates of liberalism's eternal "struggle against racism." They are ready to admit that we haven't done enough, that there is a long and difficult road ahead, in order to prevent a quick radicalization of the protests—it is not so much an increase in the violence of the protests that they fear, but their transformation into an autonomous political movement with a platform clearly demarcated from the liberal establishment. As Matthew Flisfeder wrote: "What we need to learn is not how to be post-human, but how to be equitably post-cap-italist."[23] Post-humanism is ultimately just another version of our inability to think post-capitalism: to paraphrase Fredric Jameson, it is easier to imagine all of humanity digitally inter-connected with their brains wired, sharing their experiences in a global self-awareness, than to imagine a move beyond global capitalism.

Violent protests are the return of the repressed of our lib-eral societies: a symptom that enacts what cannot be formulated in the vocabulary of liberal multiculturalism. We often criticize people for only talking instead of taking action, but the ongo-ing protests in the US are an inversion of this problem: people are acting violently because they don't have the right words to express their grievance.

To paraphrase yet again Brecht's good old saying "What is the robbing of a bank compared to the founding of a bank!," what is a direct racist obscenity compared to the obscenity of a liberal who practices multiculturalist tolerance in such a way that it allows him to retain racist prejudices? Or, as Van Jones put it on CNN:

It's not the racist white person who is in the Ku Klux Klan that we have to worry about. It's the white, liberal Hillary Clinton supporter walking her dog in Central Park who would tell you right now, "Oh I don't see race,

23. Personal communication.

race is no big deal to me, I see all people the same, I give to charities" but the minute she sees a Black man who she does not respect, or who she has a slight thought against, she weaponized race like she had been taught by the Aryan Nation.[24]

However, the example evoked by Jones is more complex. If a white woman feels uneasy when she sees a Black man approaching and clutches her bag, afraid that she will be robbed, a PC critic would accuse her of acting on her racial prejudices. To this, a new Right populist would retort that her fear was probably justified since she (or someone she knew) was likely previously robbed by a Black man—and it is not enough for the PC critic to reply that one should consider the social causes that pushed the Black man to eventually act like this. For, in seeking to deculpabilize the Black robber, the PC critic also desubjectivizes him: the robber is not guilty because he is not fully responsible for his actions but rather is a product of unfortunate circumstances (while the white racist is treated as morally fully responsible and, for this reason, despicable). It's a sad choice for the oppressed Black person: either you are subjectively deficient (according to the racist) or you are a product of objective circumstances (according to the PC liberal). How can this deadlock

24. https://www.foxnews.com/media/cnn-van-jones-white-liberal-hillary-clinton-supporter-scarier-kkk

be broken? How can blind rage be transformed into new political subjectivity?

The first step in this direction was made by some members of the police themselves. Many police officers, including NYPD chief Terence Monahan, "took the knee" alongside the protesters—a practice introduced in 2016 by American athletes during the playing of the national anthem at sporting awards ceremonies. The performance of this gesture is intended to signal the existence of racial injustice within one's country and, since it is a sign of disrespect toward the national anthem, it indicates that one is not ready to fully identify oneself with the nation—"this is not my country." It is no wonder that Chinese news outlets gleefully reported on the protests in the US, reading them as a repetition of those in Hong Kong—one of the Chinese authorities' central demands was that Hong Kong prohibit any disrespect directed at the Chinese national anthem and other state symbols.

Taking the knee also has another meaning, especially when performed by those acting on behalf of the repressive apparatus of power: it is a signal of respect for the protesters, even with a touch of self-humiliation. If we combine this meaning with the basic message, "this America (which my job requires me to act in the interests of) is not my country," we grasp the full meaning of the gesture: not a standard anti-Americanism, but a demand for a new beginning, for another America. So the recent claim of a CNN analysis, "Is the US still the world's moral leader? Not after what Trump just did this week,"[25] should be sharpened—it is now apparent that the US never was the world's moral leader since it needs a radical ethico-political renovation that far exceeds the liberal-Left's vision of tolerance.

Where, then, should we look for cases of moral leadership? There is a clear contrast here between anti-quarantine protesters and Black Lives Matter protesters: although anti-quarantine populists protest on behalf of universal freedom and dignity, while the Black Lives Matter protests also focus on the violence enacted against a particular racial group (and although some policeman probably sympathize with anti-quarantine protesters) "the idea of asking the police to join the former is laughable, despite the professed universality, whereas the latter welcomes the police support (when it is offered) even though it appears as a particular struggle."[26] In short, the "universal" anti-quarantine protests contain a unspoken bias toward white identity, while the Black Lives Matter protests are effectively universal: the only way to fight against racism in the US from a truly universal position is today to see anti-Black racism as a "singular universal," as a particular case that provides the key to universality.

I often quote an old joke from the defunct German Democratic Republic: a German worker gets a job in Siberia and,

25. https://edition.cnn.com/2020/06/06/politics/us-protests-george-floyd-world-moral-leader-intl/
26. Todd McGowan, private communication.

aware that all mail will be read by censors, he tells his friends: "Let's establish a code: if a letter you receive from me is written in ordinary blue ink, it is true; if it is written in red ink, it is false." After one month, his friends receive a letter written in blue ink that reads: "Everything is wonderful here: stores are full, food is abundant, apartments are large and properly heated, movie theatres show films from the West—the only thing unavailable is *red ink*." This is what the protest movement should seek out: the "red ink" required to properly formulate its message—or, as Ras Baraka, the mayor of Newark and son of the great Black poet Amiri Baraka, put it: we cannot win with guns; to have a chance to win, we have to use books.

Many orthodox Leftist critics dismissed my idea of a Communist prospect opened up by the ongoing pandemic with the standard Marxist argument that there is no revolution without a revolutionary party, an organized force that knows what it wants, and that such a force is, today, nowhere to be seen. However, such a critique ignores two unique features of our present predicament. First, that the situation itself—in terms of health and economy—demands measures that suspend market mechanisms and obey the maxim "to each according to his needs, from each according to his abilities," such that even conservative politicians in power are obliged to implement things close to a Universal Basic Income. Second, the global capitalist system is approaching a perfect storm in which the health crisis is combined with economic and ecological crises, international conflicts, and the anti-racist protests emerging all around the world. The combination of all of these struggles, the awareness that they are intrinsically linked, has an immense emancipatory potential.

This is why the final words of the dying Big Boss from Hideo Kojima's legendary video game *Metal Gear Solid 4: Guns of the Patriots* are today more relevant than ever: "It's not about changing the world. It's about doing our best to leave the world the way it is."[27] Today's situation calls for a new twist on this: with forests burning and Covid-19 destroying our daily lives, with widespread poverty resulting from the new riches, we have to change the world radically if we want to have even a chance of leaving it the way it is. If we do nothing, our world will soon become unrecognizable to its inhabitants. In his precise analysis, Mike Davis provides the historical background of the fires destroying vegetation across Australia:

> In the late 1940s the ruins of Berlin became a laboratory where natural scientists studied plant succession in the wake of three years of incessant fire bombing. The expectation was that the original vegetation of the region—oak woodlands and their shrubs—would soon reestablish itself. To their horror this was not the case. Instead escaped exotics, most of them alien to Germany, established themselves as the new

27. https://www.quotes.net/mquote/1040531

dominants. The persistence of this dead-zone vegetation and the failure of the plants of the Pomeranian
woodlands to reestablish themselves prompted a
debate about "Nature II." The contention was that the
extreme heat of incendiaries and the pulverization
of brick structures had created a new soil type that
invited colonization by plants such as the "tree of
heaven" (*Ailanthus*) that had evolved on the moraines
of Pleistocene ice sheets. An all-out nuclear war, they
warned, might reproduce these conditions on a vast
scale. / In the aftermath of Victoria's Black Saturday
fires in early 2009, Australian scientists calculated that
their released energy equaled the explosion of 1,500
Hiroshima-sized bombs. The current firestorms in the
Pacific states are many times larger, and we should
compare their destructive power to the mega-tonnage
of hundreds of hydrogen bombs. A new, profoundly
sinister nature is rapidly emerging from our fire rubble at the expense of landscapes we once considered
sacred. Our imaginations can barely encompass the
speed or scale of the catastrophe.[28]

We (humanity, i.e. our mode of production) are not just "destroying nature," we are co-creating a new nature in which there will
be no place for us. And is the ongoing pandemic not an exemplary case of "a new, profoundly sinister nature"? We shouldn't,

28. https://rosaluxnycblog.org/california-fires/

therefore, worry too much about the survival of nature, of natural forms of life on Earth—nature will survive, only changed beyond OUR recognition.

The crucial trap to be avoided here is to conclude that, since we are facing a multidimensional global crisis, particular interventions are not enough—that a kind of radical ethical change, a new global ethics, is needed. Those in power like such calls for new ethics, as they seem to provide a simple way out of a crisis; they love to conceive of a crisis as a largely ethical problem (remember that, back in 2008, the Vatican was quick to comment that the crisis was not one of capitalist finance but one of ethics). What is needed today is for us to develop a clear perception of all the dimensions of the crisis we are in, without privileging one aspect over the other (like those who claim that in our struggle against the pandemic we have the right to neglect the ecological crisis), and for radical social change to follow from this: action should follow thinking.

Slavoj Žižek is one of the most prolific and well-known philosophers and cultural theorists in the world today. His inventive, provocative body of work mixes Hegelian metaphysics, Lacanian psychoanalysis, and Marxist dialectic in order to challenge conventional wisdom and accepted verities on both the Left and the Right.